*Essays on Modern European Revolutionary History*

*The Walter Prescott Webb Memorial Lectures:* XI
Sponsored by The University of Texas at Arlington

# The Walter Prescott Webb Memorial Lectures

*Essays on Modern European Revolutionary History*

By
Stanley H. Palmer
Anthony S. Baker
Dennis Reinhartz
R. R. Palmer
George Barr Carson, Jr.

*Introduction by Charles Tilly*
*Edited by Bede K. Lackner and Kenneth Roy Philp*

University of Texas Press    Austin & London

D
359.7
.E84

*Library of Congress Cataloging in Publication Data*
Main entry under title:
Essays on modern European revolutionary history.
  (The Walter Prescott Webb memorial lectures; 11 ISSN
0083–713X)
  1. Revolutions—Addresses, essays, lectures. 2. Revolutionists—
Addresses, essays, lectures. 3. Europe—History—19th century—
Addresses, essays, lectures. 4. Europe—History—20th century—
Addresses, essays, lectures. I. Palmer, Stanley H. II. Lackner, Bede K.
III. Philp, Kenneth R., 1941–   IV. Series: The Walter Prescott Webb
memorial lectures; 11.
D359.7E84        940.2'8      76–43976
ISBN 0–292–72021–1

*In Memory of Harold M. Hollingsworth*

# Contents

# Preface

On April 1, 1976, the eleventh annual Walter Prescott Webb Memorial Lectures were held at the University of Texas at Arlington. Much
has been written about Walter Prescott Webb and his work, and such
tributes ordinarily do full justice to a man of stature. But we are confronted with a greatness that calls for a continued probing of his
legacy and the resolve to advance on the path outlined by his genius.
The bicentennial of our Republic opportunely suggests "revolution"
as a topic. This theme would have pleased Webb because it transcends
narrow confines and opens up new and wider horizons. Accordingly,
this year's lectures investigate the diverse facets of modern European
revolutionary history which sought to bring about a worthy life. Fol-

lowing the format of previous years, members of the University of Texas at Arlington history faculty presented papers during the morning, while a distinguished visiting historian delivered the evening lecture.

Professor Stanley H. Palmer reviews the epic struggle of the Irish nation in the first decades of the nineteenth century which involved economic, religious, and political aspirations for freedom, often against overwhelming odds. Under the enlightened leadership of Daniel O'Connell, a Catholic lawyer, the principle of nonviolent resistance was used to improve the condition of the Irish peasantry and to ensure the success of future generations. The legacy of Fernand Pelloutier, who influenced the French trade union movement of the 1890s, is examined by Professor Anthony S. Baker. Pelloutier, an organizational genius, stressed the need for a responsible working class free from the shackles of self-serving exploiters. But his advocacy of revolutionary syndicalism and the general strike was marred by an inadequate understanding of economic theory.

Professor Dennis Reinhartz probes the ideological transformation of Milovan Djilas, one of the leaders of the Yugoslav Communist Revolution. In his devotion to human justice, Djilas passionately espoused the great ideologies of the East, only to withdraw, decades later, in disappointment when his ideas were betrayed by intolerance, greed, and the lack of true revolutionary fervor which robbed him of his most prized possessions—his Montenegrine roots and his soul. The featured speaker, Professor R. R. Palmer, of Yale University, shows how European revolutionaries have viewed the American Revolution. All will agree that 1776 was an inspiration to Europe in the first half of the nineteenth century, but things changed when *revolution, democracy*, and *revolutionary socialism* acquired an altogether radical meaning. Thus the aspirations of the Founding Fathers lost their appeal to the European Left, even though the United States remains a land of opportunity, technological innovation, and equality down to the present day.

In 1976, the University of Texas at Arlington sponsored its second Webb-Smith essay competition, funded by a generous grant from C. B. Smith of Austin. The award is given each year for the best paper submitted on the topic of the lectures. The current winner is George Barr Carson, Jr., of Oregon State University, whose "National

Sovereignty at the Bar: Revolution by Law?" examines how the Court of Justice of the European Communities continued one aspect of the revolutionary experience by challenging the unlimited sovereignty of the nation-state. The Court of Justice has not only upheld the natural rights of individuals irrespective of national boundaries; it has also opened the door to a greater future for Europe in which the American idea of *E pluribus unum* is slowly but surely becoming a reality. Professor Carson's essay is included with the papers delivered during the lectures.

As usual, the Webb Lectures Committee would like to thank all participants in the series—speakers, students, faculty, and the staff of the Press—for their help and cooperation.

This volume is dedicated to Harold M. Hollingsworth, who died on September 8, 1975. Harold received his Ph.D. from the University of Tennessee and taught at Mary Hardin-Baylor College before joining the history faculty at Arlington in 1963. He quickly demonstrated his professional commitment by suggesting that the history department inaugurate an annual series of lectures to honor Walter Prescott Webb. Harold edited four volumes of the lectures before accepting a position to teach American constitutional and legal history at Wright State University in Dayton, Ohio. He showed great fortitude in a cruel and painful illness which took him much too soon, in the best years of his life and academic career. A lively thinker, outstanding teacher, delightful conversationalist, and true friend to his students and colleagues, Harold M. Hollingsworth will be missed by all who knew him.

Bede K. Lackner
Kenneth Roy Philp

*Introduction*
Charles Tilly

"To complain of the age we live in," wrote Edmund Burke in 1770, "to murmur at the present possessors of power, to lament the past, to conceive extravagant hopes of the future, are the common dispositions of the greatest part of mankind; indeed, the necessary effects of the ignorance and levity of the vulgar. Such complaints and humours have existed in all times; yet as all times have *not* been alike, true political sagacity manifests itself in distinguishing that complaint which only characterizes the general infirmity of human nature, from those which are symptoms of the particular distemperature of our own air and season."

Yet, declared Burke, the current circumstances really were exceptionally alarming:

*That government is at once dreaded and condemned; that the laws
are despoiled of all their respected and salutary terrors; that their
inaction is a subject of ridicule, and their exertion of abhorrence;
that rank, and office, and title, and all the solemn plausibilities of the
world, have lost their reverence and effect; that our foreign politics
are as much deranged as our domestic economy; that our dependen-
cies are slackened in their affection, and loosened from their obedience; that we know neither how to yield nor how to enforce; that
hardly anything above or below, abroad or at home, is sound and
entire; but that disconnection and confusion, in offices, in parties, in
families, in parliament, in the nation, prevail beyond the disorders
of any former time: these are facts universally admitted and lamented.* (Thoughts on the Cause of the Present Discontents)

The rhetoric is familiar. Only the Burkean elegance distinguishes it
from thousands of other political laments. Things are falling apart,
government has lost its grip. We might think that Burke had fallen
prey to the vulgar illusion he had just condemned.

We cannot, however, dismiss Burke's analysis as mere rhetoric or
conservative nostalgia. Such analyses as his do often preface excoria-
tions of the mob, pleas for renewed faith, demands that strong government step in. But Burke went another way. "When popular
discontents have been very prevalent," he wrote, "it may well be
affirmed and supported, that there has been generally something
found amiss in the constitution, or in the conduct of Government.
The people have no interest in disorder." The object of Burke's indig-
nation was the governing group of "king's friends" clustered around
Lord Bute. Bute's faction had, in Burke's analysis, not only pursued
stupid policies. It had also weakened the government by disregarding
the will of Parliament and of the people. Burke found the resulting
foreign and colonial policy to be a disaster. In previous years he had
often argued the American case against the claims of the Crown. At
home, he complained about the treatment of John Wilkes, the popular
hero whom the government had imprisoned for his attacks on royal

policy, convicted for possession of licentious publications, and then arranged to have excluded from Parliament after his election from Middlesex.

For about five years, crowds in London and in the American colonies had often acted out their own discontent by displaying and destroying a large boot. "Boot" meant "Bute." During the Stamp Act crisis of 1765–66 American protesters and their English sympathizers commonly blamed the objectionable colonial policies on Bute. In Charleston, South Carolina, for example:

*A gallows was erected, on which the Effigies of a Stamp man, the Devil, and the Head of Lord B——e, in a Boot, were suspended. On the Gallows these Words were affixed; "Liberty and no Stamp-Act." The Stamp man hung in the Center, with this Advertisement on his breast: "Stamp Paper sold here for ready Money only." On his Back, "He who dare pull this down, had better have a Mill-Stone tied about his Neck, and cast into the Sea." At the Back of the Stamp-man was placed the Devil, with this Label in his Hand; "Push in, S——y, ruin your Country, for Money is your Major." Lord B——e's head in a Boot graced the Front, with these Words round the Neck, "Behold, my Countrymen, the just Reward of a Bad Minister." (Boston Gazette and Country Journal, November 11, 1765)*

"S——y" was George Saxby, the designated stamp collector for South Carolina. "Lord B——e" was Burke's enemy, the king's friend Lord Bute. The pageantry of protest against the Stamp Act had originated in New England and spread rapidly throughout the American colonies. But the same symbolism appeared in ceremonies staged by Wilkes's supporters back in London. Thus Edmund Burke found himself in alliance, if not in complete agreement, with John Wilkes, Samuel Adams, and the crowds of London and Boston.

That odd alliance would be enough to qualify the 1760s and 1770s as a time of unusual political conflict. There is more. In America, in England, and in the rest of Europe the end of the Seven Years' War in 1763 left winners and losers alike with the problem of absorbing the costs of the war. The costs were both financial and political. In the Netherlands and France, for example, military and fiscal losses rapidly became severe political liabilities for the current regimes. In England and America, three major results of the war occasioned deep political divisions. The first was the absorption of conquered Catholic Quebec, with a special religious status, into a Protestant-run empire. The second was the great expense of the war. The third was the large continuing cost of the North American military establishment which issued from the war and guarded Britain's greatly expanded American frontiers. The fiscal expedients—such as the Stamp Act—adopted by the British contributed powerfully to the development of colonial opposition. The colonial opposition turned into the American Revolution.

The international connections are fascinating. For example, the French government, still staggering under the debts incurred during the Seven Years' War against England, undertook a costly military alliance with the rebellious Americans. That financial burden led to the calling of the 1789 Estates General. The Estates General became the initial instrument of France's great revolution. This does not mean, to be sure, that the Seven Years' War "caused" the French Revolution. It does mean that multiple threads ran among the numerous conflicts, domestic and international, which agitated the later eighteenth century. The French experience also illustrates the importance of the cost of growing armies and expanding states to the creation of eighteenth-century revolutionary situations. In that context, we begin to understand why fiscal problems and resistance to taxation figure so prominently in the great rebellions of the century.

Burke, writing in 1770, justified himself by appeal to a revolutionary tradition. The revolution in question, however, was the Glorious Revolution of 1688. That revolution, in his view, confirmed a constitution in which Parliament spoke for the people, and the king was obliged to listen. He condemned the king's friends for violating the constitution and betraying the revolution. Before the American and French revolutions, therefore, the search for political legitimacy in a revolutionary tradition had already begun.

In the two succeeding centuries, we have become accustomed to the idea that our own is the true age of revolution. The word *revolution* has prestige; authors and politicians will manipulate its definition in order to include the changes of which they approve and to eliminate those of which they disapprove. As a result, the word has many meanings: not only the Glorious Revolution and the American

Revolution, but the Industrial Revolution and the Sexual Revolution as well.

The papers in this volume illustrate the variety of available definitions. By implication or by declaration, all of them concern revolutions or revolutionaries. Stanley H. Palmer writes of Irish struggles against the British and for control of the land. Anthony S. Baker and Dennis Reinhartz discuss important leaders of revolutionary movements: the French Fernand Pelloutier and the Yugoslav Milovan Djilas. R. R. Palmer reviews the changing place of the American Revolution in western views of revolutionary possibilities. Finally, George Barr Carson, Jr., analyzing conflicts between national and international law in the European Communities, locates the kernel of the European revolutionary tradition not in the violent overthrow of governments but in the introduction—however peaceful—of radical change.

No single definition of revolution will neatly unite these diverse topics and yet separate them from the bulk of western political life. In fact, their diversity is twofold: it consists partly in varying notions of revolution as such and partly in the singling out of different aspects of revolutionary phenomena. At least three aspects of revolution compete for attention. The first is the development of revolutionary *situations*, in the form of deep conflicts and division, whatever their origins and outcomes. The second is the production of revolutionary *changes*, however they come about. The third is the creation of revolutionary *outlooks*, in the form of intentions to transform the world at any cost, whether or not those outlooks coincide with revolutionary situations and promote revolutionary changes.

We commonly think of revolutionary situations, changes, and outlooks as highly interdependent. For example, one standard formulation has deep divisions emerging from economic crises and promoting the spread of revolutionary ideas and resentments, which in their turn motivate people to rise up, seize power, and transform their world. Yet revolutionary situations, outlooks, and changes have no necessary connection with each other. Most analysts of revolution, indeed, spend a good deal of their time considering the circumstances in which revolutionary situations and/or outlooks arise without leading to revolutionary changes. The sharpest debates concern whether revolutionary changes can occur in the absence of revolutionary situations and outlooks. Conservatives tend to say yes, radicals no. Thus divergences of definition lead back to divergences of political philosophy and strategy.

These essays on modern European revolutionary history generally pay little explicit attention to definitions and statements of political philosophy. They move immediately into the business of analyzing particular events, movements, people, and conflicts. Stanley Palmer is concerned, not with general theories of revolution, but with the changing efforts of Irish countrymen to cast off British rule and regain control over their soil. The Irish Rebellion of 1798, the retributive justice of the Whiteboys, Daniel O'Connell's campaign for Catholic Emancipation, the Tithe War of the 1830s all pass in review. Then Palmer shows us their gains dissolving in the famine of the 1840s. Despite that dissolution, Palmer notes the enduring double legacy of the nineteenth-cenury Irish movement: the creation of a set of ideas justifying and promoting the participation of all Irishmen in a unified national resistance; the widely imitated use of associations, demonstrations, and nonviolent displays of moral force to place pressure on governments.

Anthony Baker's essay on Fernand Pelloutier traces the short, intense public life of one of the great organizers of French revolutionary syndicalism. Pelloutier died in 1901, burned out by work and disease at the age of thirty-three. In the previous decade he had played a major part in the creation of two distinctive features of the French labor movement of his time: the great importance of the Bourses du Travail—local "labor exchanges" uniting the organizations of different trades—in working-class political and economic action; the belief in the general strike as a means of accomplishing working-class ends and, especially, of making a proletarian revolution. Whether we consider the outcome of his efforts tragic or merely ironic depends on how realistic we consider his original program to have been. The labor exchanges did become durable, influential centers for mutual aid, political education, and strike activity; a kind of short, general strike did become a standard means by which organized French workers put pressure on employers and government. The tragedy, or irony, lies in the fact that both institutions gave workers an investment in the existing political and economic arrangements. That is not what the revolutionary Pelloutier had in mind.

With Milovan Djilas we come to a contemporary hero. Indeed, Dennis Reinhartz bases some of his sketch of Djilas on his own recent conversations with the Yugoslav revolutionary leader. The sketch accents two themes: how Djilas became a revolutionary; how Djilas stopped being a Stalinist. We see Djilas as a Montenegrin nationalist and self-made socialist who gradually changed his views about the proper means of advancing those constant ends. At the end, Reinhartz sets us to wondering to what degree and in what sense Djilas— "groping for a Tolstoyan-Gandhian worldview to provide a counter-reality to Montenegro"—is still a revolutionary.

R. R. Palmer takes us back to the eighteenth century with observations on the changing European reputation of the American Revolution. Just as it seems a little odd two centuries later that Edmund Burke should have used the Glorious Revolution as his reference point, it is a bit difficult for twentieth-century observers to appreciate the former importance of the American Revolution as a demonstration of the possibility of successful rebellion against an unjust government. Disillusion has intervened. In Palmer's analysis, the French Revolution of 1789–1799 dimmed the American example by going farther, and doing so more dramatically. To some degree the themes of liberty, equality, and fraternity permeated both revolutions. But the Americans gave a greater emphasis to liberty, the French (at least the French of 1793–04) to equality. Since then, Palmer tells us, European revolutions and revolutionaries have stressed egalitarian democracy. Thus they may take for granted the libertarian gains of the American Revolution, but they do not value those gains highly. The subsequent emergence of the United States as a wealthy, self-satisfied international power showing little promise of a working-class revolution made the American example all the less attractive to European revolutionaries, whatever their views of the eighteenth-century struggle.

"National Sovereignty at the Bar: Revolution by Law?" is George Barr Carson's challenge to conventional conceptions of revolution. For two or three hundred years, the main flow of western history has led us toward increasing national sovereignty, growing priority of the rights and powers of national states over those of any other social units—individuals, families, local communities, churches, even business firms. Since World War II, however, two countertrends have assumed importance. One is the growth of corporations and commercial combines so big and sprawling as to rival, or even to envelop, some of the states within whose territories they operate. The other is the proliferation, strengthening, and regularization of international blocs and federations; the blocs and federations typically begin with member states but acquire autonomous power.

Carson stresses the second antinational trend. He calls our attention to the creation of a body of international law by the courts of the European Communities. The principle of equal treatment across all members of the Communities becomes a tool by which the international tribunals chip away at the laws and prerogatives of individual states. On his way to that analysis of the contemporary scene, Carson fashions a detailed, controversial discussion of the importance of property rights to the liberty of the revolutionary trilogy. That discussion takes us back to contemporary international law because the major rationale of the antinational decisions, in Carson's view, is that unequal treatment deprives people of property, in a broad sense of the term. It is a nice turn of the dialectic. The seeming antithesis of revolution—the creeping, wordy travel of lawsuits through the courts—depends intimately on the work of previous revolutions. If Carson is right, it even produces a new revolution: a long, slow murmur rather than a sudden shout, but the more profound because of its thoroughness.

We have before us, then, a set of American reflections on the European revolutionary scene. The reflections range from the eighteenth century to the twentieth. They differ in their implicit estimates of the possibility, the desirability, the very essence of revolution. They vary in their emphasis on revolutionary situations, revolutionary changes, and revolutionary outlooks. Yet they stand out from any likely European collection on the same subject in several regards. Their tone is, on the whole, cool and pragmatic. We encounter no complex terminology or formidable models of revolution. No author makes a deliberate effort to build up or tear down a Marxist analysis. We hear almost nothing explicit about capitalism, industrialism, and their transformations. Political problems and processes preoccupy us.

The strong emphasis on politics provides a welcome complement to the numerous analyses of revolution which leap from economic discontent to revolutionary struggle without analyzing the organization, mobilization, and collective action which links the two. It provides a convincing counter to the frequent assumption that mass action occurs in a wild world apart from routine politics. Like Edmund Burke, the authors of *Essays on Modern European Revolutionary History* suppose that European crowds and European revolutionaries usually knew what they wanted, however often they failed to achieve their ends. Like Burke, our authors see significant continuities between revolutionary politics and politics as usual. By analyzing revolutionary situations, changes, and outlook, they tell us, we can better understand the political alternatives, revolutionary and nonrevolutionary, actually before us.

*Essays on Modern European Revolutionary History*

# Rebellion, Emancipation, Starvation: The Dilemma of Peaceful Protest in Ireland, 1798–1848

*Stanley H. Palmer*

*As to the Repeal question, it is merely a catchy word. Yesterday, the cry was "Emancipation"; to day, it is, "Tithes" and "Repeal"; tomorrow, it will be something else. And thus will the passions of the people be kept boiling over until, at some favourable opportunity, an effort will be made to throw off English connection, and a free and undisguised license be granted for the open indulgence of long cherished rancour and bitterness towards England.*
—Police report, 1832[1]

The great Irish Rebellion of 1798 was short and bloody. It claimed more lives in two months than the guillotine did in France during the

Reign of Terror in 1793 and 1794. Conceived by its leaders as a war for independence from England, the Irish Rebellion quickly degenerated into a civil war of peculiar savagery. The pitched battles saw desperate and brutal fighting. At Carlow, British troops lured 1,500 attacking rebels into ambush and killed 600. At Enniscorthy, 6,000 rebels killed 80 soldiers in a three-hour battle and put to flight the remaining 200. At New Ross, the rebels failed to occupy the town after vicious fighting which took the lives of more than 200 troops and 2,000 peasants. They failed, too, to take Arklow, leaving 1,000 dead after a five-hour battle. This turned the tide, and in late June, General Gerard Lake and an army of 13,000 captured the rebel headquarters at Vinegar Hill, killing 600 of the defenders.

More deaths in the rebellion resulted from atrocities than from wounds in battle. The British used a special torture called "the pitch cap," in which hot pitch tar was applied to a shaven head; occasionally, gunpowder was applied first, and the victim dispatched to eternity. The government seldom gave quarter to rebel prisoners: one improvised means of execution was a crude device on wheels known as the "Traveling Gallows." British troops shot men, women and children, unarmed and in the act of surrendering. The soldiers stripped, mutilated, and sometimes disemboweled bodies. They raped countless women, put entire villages to the torch, and systematically razed Catholic chapels. Years afterward, the peasantry would flee in terror at the very sight of a British uniform.

The rebels committed their own atrocities. They set fire to a military barracks in county Kildare, killing 80 soldiers inside—some being skewered on long iron-tipped sticks, known as pikes, as they tried to escape the flames. At Vinegar Hill, the rebels subjected 500 Protestant prisoners to mock trials culminating in executions by guns, pikes, and floggings. At Scullabogue, upon news of a military defeat, Irish rebels set fire to a barn containing 184 Protestant prisoners, all of whom perished. After a rebel party occupied Wexford, 97 Protestants were, over a three-hour period, piked to death on the town's bridge and then tossed into the river below.[2]

The total loss of life in the Irish Rebellion was about 30,000 persons, of whom only 1,600 were the king's soldiers.[3] Property losses were incalculable. The government officially executed 81 persons for treason and shipped 1,800 prisoners overseas to the West Indies, Australia, and the salt mines of Prussia.[4] Finally, almost as an anticlimax, the English in 1801 formally annexed Ireland to form a part of the new Union of Great Britain and Ireland.

In the long view, the rebellion was but one event in the history of an island drenched in violence. In the 1650s, Oliver Cromwell had taken some eight million acres—half the cultivable land—from the Catholics and given them to Irish Protestants and, above all, to English merchants, mercenaries, and adventurers. He forced the dispossessed, in the famous violent phrase, to go to "Hell or Connaught."[5]

The barbarous nature of the confiscation, fueled by religious and nationalist considerations, kept the Cromwellian settlement alive in the popular mind. In 1825, Colonel John Irwin, a county Sligo magistrate, tried to explain to a parliamentary committee the nature of agrarian discontent in Ireland. He recalled that one of his trusted gardeners, a man who had joined the rebels in 1798, had once stated that the property was really his, since he was "descended from the family whom Oliver Cromwell [had] dispossessed." Colonel Irwin also told the committee that, as a boy of ten, he had heard a similar protest from a Catholic tutor who often told him, "I ought to be in possession of these walks that we are now amusing ourselves in." Indeed, Irwin continued, "within these two years [from 1823 to 1825] that same individual (he is now, I understand, dead), but with one foot then in the grave, told me the same thing, and I suppose it was not to me alone that he told it; he most likely told it to his son. I only tell the Committee what is the feeling."[6] In 1852 another investigating committee asked a witness for his solution to the agrarian problem. He replied: "I do not know of any change short of a perfect confiscation that would give satisfaction. . . . There is a great deal of feeling among the lower orders of Roman Catholics that they are the owners . . . of the soil. . . . Some of them keep maps of the estates which they consider they ought to have."[7]

After the Cromwellian settlement came the political and social legislation of William and Anne.[8] The Penal Laws reduced the Catholic Irish, in Edmund Burke's words, to "a race of savages who were a disgrace to human nature itself." Catholics could not vote, hold public office, or receive any kind of education. They could not worship in buildings with steeples, bells, or even crosses. Possession of such weapons as pikes and muskets became a criminal offense. Harsh property laws deprived Catholics not only of the right to freehold of land but also of lifelong leases and property inheritance. According to an Irish chief justice, "The law does not suppose any such person to exist as an Irish Roman Catholic."[9]

Few opinions of the nonpersons are extant. Aodhagán Ó Rathaille (ca. 1670–1726), who grew up near Killarney when the memory of Cromwell was still fresh, called Ireland,

*A land of fetters—it is sickness to me unto death!*
*A land which wolves have spitefully devoured!*
*A land placed in misfortune and subjection*
*Beneath the tyranny of enemies and mercenaries and robbers!*
*A land without produce or thing of worth of any kind!*
*A land stripped naked, without shelter or boughs!*
*A land broken down by the English-prating band!*

Another poet, Sean Clárach MacDomhnaill, active before 1750, heartily wished all Saxons "tourment and gripping fever / in the heat of hellfire." By midcentury, the British relaxed enforcement of the Penal Laws, but the oppression and stigma remained, as Eoghan Ruadh, a Munster bard, lamented:

*'Tis not the poverty I most detest*
*Nor being down for ever,*
*But the insult that follows it,*
*Which no leeches can cure.*[10]

This lax application of the Penal Laws eventually led to repeal of certain disabilities. After 1778, Catholics could take lifelong leases; after 1793, they could vote on the same terms as Protestants, bear arms if they met a property qualification, and hold all but the highest civil and military offices. But the poverty and the stigma of being a native Irishman remained. As early as 1780, Arthur Young, an English agriculturist, noted that the effect of the Penal Laws was not so much against Catholicism, "but against the industry and property of whoever professes that religion." Visiting Englishman Edward Wakefield noted in 1812 that in heavily Catholic county Mayo "the term

Catholic is not a mark of religious distinction, but of every other distinction whatever."[11]

"Papist," a witness told a parliamentary committee in 1825, is a word constantly in the mouths of lower-class Protestants: "The degradation with which it is supposed to be attended, excites feelings of the deepest animosity among the people." After killing an old man, a drunken Protestant policeman yelled, "There is not a popish Dog in the street I will not give the same sauce to." Newspaper advertisements were invariably signed, "Prot.," a practice "extremely galling to the Roman Catholic." An Irish commissioner of education reported that Catholics, of whatever economic level, feel part of "a degraded class," and "do not consider that a Protestant and a Catholic stand upon equal [levels] whenever questions arise between them." The head agent of one of the largest estates in the country put it simply: a Catholic "is considered by a Protestant *of the same class*, as inferior to him, and I think that has a great effect upon his conduct and manners."[12]

The Protestant Anglo-Irish themselves were not masters of their fate. Even before the Union, the Irish Parliament acted only on laws prepared by London-appointed governors, the lord lieutenant and chief secretary, in Dublin Castle. This Irish Catholic and Protestant dependency on England was economic as well as political. Until 1780, the entire nation suffered under laws which crippled trade and industry. Opening Irish commerce to world markets after that date brought little relief. Her small capital stock, tiny entrepreneurial class, poor communications, absence of towns, and undisciplined labor force meant that Ireland could not compete with industrializing urban England. When coal and iron became the sinews of modernization, the country, with its meager mineral resources, was cursed by nature as well as history.[13]

Ireland was overwhelmingly agrarian. As late as 1840, when England had seventy-one towns of 10,000 or more population, Ireland had eight; 33 percent of the English population lived in towns larger than 20,000, while in Ireland 8 percent of the population resided in settlements half that size.[14] Forty-five percent of the agricultural holdings in Ireland in 1840 were five acres or smaller, and 92 percent of the agricultural population consisted of laborers or small tenant farmers.[15]

Most of the tenantry paid their rents to land agents or middlemen holding long leases from absentee landlords. Often there were several middlemen, each leasing for a shorter period and at a higher rent to someone below him. Characteristically, the occupier-farmer, his morsel of land already encumbered with rent, taxes, and tithe, aggravated the situation by subdividing his tenancy among his sons upon their marriage.

Despite this unproductive system, the peasantry, subsisting on the potato staple, increased from three to six million persons in the seventy years after 1750. In the absence of towns and industries, the Irish clung to the land. Untouched by an agricultural revolution and without a system of poor relief until 1838, Ireland was a country with a single obsession: the land question. Its two principal components were rent and tithe. Population pressures on the cultivable soil, combined with desires by landlords and land agents for quick profits, produced a revolving-door effect of rent increases accompanied by tenant evictions. Tithing, or payments in kind by the tenantry of about one-tenth of the annual crop, provided another grievance. These tithes were paid to the Anglican Church of Ireland; its collectors, the tithe proctors, were, with the middlemen or land agents, the persons most hated by the Catholic peasantry.[16]

Stripped of landownership, uneducated, lacking political rights, and scorned as papists, the Irish peasantry turned within itself for strength. Secret societies appeared as early as 1760 but probably go back even earlier; an observer in 1832 described their purposes and activities as being "of the same kind for the last sixty years."[17] Known locally by various names, but collectively described as "Whiteboys" (from the group practice of wearing white hats or shirts), they were bands of night riders, usually strangers from another part of the county or from another county, who inflicted retributive justice against persons representative of the oppressive land system. Whiteboy grievances concerned rent and tithes rather than political or religious questions. Their victims were Catholics as well as Protestants. The Whiteboys visited tithe proctors and middlemen, who were usually of the reformed religion, but they also harassed Catholic tenant farmers who evicted occupying leaseholders and even Catholic priests who exacted high fees from their parishioners.[18]

Like English food rioters, the Whiteboys acted within a strict ritualistic code of behavior. Both English and Irish rioters gave notice to their victims, but the Whiteboys went one important step beyond the English bread rioters who had seized grain, slit the sacks, and occasionally burned flour mills.[19] The Irish night riders destroyed property but also physically injured their victims. Stories circulated of persons buried up to their chins in graves lined with furze or briars, or of victims made to ride naked on horseback on saddles of thorns. Occasionally, Whiteboys cut off one or both of a man's ears; sometimes they burned people in shirts tarred with pitch, or they ripped out eyes and tongues. Peculiar to Meath and Westmeath until about 1820 was "carding," a severe and rarely employed torture in which the victim's back was shredded by stroking a wool card (a small board filled with iron spikes) across his skin, sometimes in intricate and fatal diamond patterns. Occasionally, Whiteboys used powerful psychological tortures, such as the raping of women "in order to wreak vengeance on their husbands or fathers" who were forced to witness the outrage. Much more common was property damage and personal beatings, the violence occasionally culminating in murder, either by premeditation or by sheer excess of punishment. Whiteboy activities were usually nocturnal, but daytime assassinations, sometimes before large numbers of spectators, were not unheard-of.[20]

The spectacular nature of Whiteboy crime made good newspaper copy but masked the motives underlying the protest. Most Irish Protestants were content to deplore the "outrages" of the native savages. But one Englishman, George Cornewall Lewis, understood the movement.[21] In a remarkable book published in 1836, Lewis concluded that the Whiteboys were "administrators of a law of opinion" commonly held among the numerous small tenant farmers and laborers. He described the movement as "a vast trades union for the protection of the Irish peasantry." The Whiteboy, who lived by secrecy, obedience, and personal self-denial manifested in sworn oaths, viewed himself as a judge, not a criminal. To him the crime was the agricultural system and the society in which he lived. He rejected the laws of the state and imposed peasant law codes in their place. Breaking Whiteboy law resulted only in sanctions as painful as those employed by the criminal law—namely, loss of property, corporal punishment, or death. Whiteboys, Lewis noted, "do not seek for indiscriminate plunder, they desire not a general sack, but a new tenure of property: they wish to substitute *one* government for *another*, but not to produce *anarchy*. They are . . . conscious that if each man . . . abandons the common cause, they themselves may fall a prey to the universal scramble."[22]

Crime in Ireland was thus fundamentally different from crime in England. Personal, individual, self-serving actions characterized law-breaking in England; impersonal, collective, "exemplary or prevent-ive" behavior marked Irish crime. As early as 1787 a member of the Irish Parliament noted that "a new power . . . in the land seemed to have more real strength than the legislature ever had. This royal Will-o'-the-Wisp, whom no man could catch, made laws infinitely more effectual or better enforced, than those of parliament." In 1834, the lord lieutenant, the Marquess Wellesley, concluded, "It is more safe to violate the law than to obey it."[23] In 1852, a Protestant Irishman, in explaining to Parliament the difficulty of enforcing the law in his country, observed that "in Ireland, crime is generally, somehow or other, the crime of the community, whereas in England it is the crime of an individual."[24]

Between 1822 and 1835 relative criminal activity in Ireland, re-flected in total prisoner committals, was twice as high as in England. Executions in Ireland for murder were per capita three times greater than in England. During the period 1834–1849 offenses against per-sons and property committed with violence were per capita two times greater in Ireland than in England.[25]

To combat this widespread agrarian "outrage" the English govern-ment maintained an imposing array of physical force. A militia was established in 1793, and three years later, a part-time cavalry force, the heavily Protestant Yeomanry. About twenty thousand regular British troops, infantry and cavalry, were scattered in detachments across the countryside. After the rebellion in 1798, the English gov-ernment took over and expanded the police force in Dublin. Begin-ning in 1814, the local police were supplanted in a few counties by government squads of riot police. Because hardship and hunger con-tinued to produce intense Whiteboyism, the government responded in 1822 by creating an armed constabulary in all thirty-two counties.[26]

The failure of these recent Whiteboy protests and the creation of a rural police left the Irish peasantry in a mood of sullen apathy. This artificial peace would probably have continued, broken only by outbreaks of terrorism, had it not been for the brilliant idea of a young Catholic lawyer.[27] The Union of Great Britain and Ireland had been consummated on the promise that Catholics would be allowed to sit as members of Parliament in London. George III, however, had vetoed the proposal, and lobbying efforts by the Catholic Association, a small group of middle-class Catholics, failed to enact that promise. In early 1824, the young lawyer, Daniel O'Connell, decided to bring the issue to the Irish masses. His idea was to offer membership in the Catholic Association on the installment plan. He lowered Association dues to a shilling a year and permitted payments of one penny a month. This "Catholic Rent" was an immediate political success. Donated at Sunday services all over Ireland and collected by the clergy, the Catholic Rent soon brought in a thousand pounds sterling a month. By March 1825, £16,200 were collected; by 1829, a total of £52,300.[28]

It was not the amount which troubled the authorities, although, as one Anglo-Irishman observed, with two pence a month the Catholics would "have the means of levying war, or doing what else they please." Rather, "it was the principle of the thing." The Catholic Rent was "the wickedest contrivance of mischief . . . the most dangerous invention, and the most efficient thing, too, that has ever been thought of by the disturbers of that country."[29] Inspector-General of Police George Warburton agreed: "It brings the lowest person in the scale of that persuasion almost into contact with the highest, and . . . forms a stronger bond of union, perhaps, than anything which has occurred in my recollection."[30] Between this new alliance of "the higher classes" and the "very low" was a "middle class . . . influenced by radical principles . . . who did not at all apply themselves to political concerns before." Committees, branching out from the Catholic Association, created in "little country towns and country villages" a unanimity of Catholic opinion. Handbills, pamphlets, and newspapers, "read by one individual to a great many," told the people of their oppression.[31] "The People say that they have only just learned their Rights," a Protestant nobleman gloomily informed Dublin Castle in 1826. "I don't think that I am an Alarmist, but I must say that I never saw such a change in the Mind of any body of People as has been effected . . . in this country."[32]

If the change was remarkable, it was also a bit mystifying. Many Catholic tenant farmers had had the vote since 1793.[33] "Emancipation," as the movement defined its aims, really involved allowing Catholics to sit as members of Parliament: but no peasant subsisting on a few acres of potatoes could, in his wildest dreams, imagine himself in the House of Commons. On the other hand, he could sense the importance of having a representative of his own religion there. Bishop James Doyle told a parliamentary committee in 1825 that the lower-class Catholics felt it a mark of infamy that their higher-class coreligionists were excluded from seats in Parliament. Daniel O'Connell went so far as to tell the same gentlemen that he had heard peasants say that Emancipation would greatly benefit their children, who would enjoy rights which they had never had.[34]

The movement thus had both a practical and a symbolic appeal. On the one hand, members of Parliament were now being defined as directly representative of a constituency, rather than responsible only to themselves in the Burkean concept of virtual representation. Symbolically, on the other hand, Emancipation stood for much more. The liberal measures of the last quarter of the eighteenth century had raised the level of general expectation throughout the peasantry. Injustices, once tolerated, became unacceptable by the 1820s. The peasants' inability to specify a particular instance of political oppression only served to give Emancipation a symbolic importance. Many do not "know exactly" their disabilities, observed an Irish magistrate, but "they know there is a disqualification, and that they feel it." A Catholic bishop described the peasants' view of Emancipation: "They perhaps would not be able to define it, but they have a feeling that they are belonging to an excluded cast[e]. . . . They are anxious to be relieved from this kind of slavery, which they are not able to explain."[35]

The political awakening of the masses was accompanied by another new force in politics, the Roman Catholic clergy. Earlier peasant movements had existed independently of the priests; O'Connell's relied on them. Foes and advocates of Emancipation agreed on the new importance of the Church. "It is impossible to detail to you in a letter," Chief Secretary Henry Goulburn wrote Home Secretary Robert Peel, "the various modes in which the Roman Catholic priesthood now interfere in every transaction of every description. . . . In many parts of the country their services are purely political and the altars in the several chapels, instead of being used as they used to be for disseminating the general doctrines of Christianity or the peculiar tenets of their faith, are the rostra from which they declaim on the subject of Roman Catholic grievances, exhort to the collection of [the Catholic] rent, or denounce their Protestant neighbours."[36]

The priests injected a partisan note into the political radicalism. In sermons they counseled parishioners to boycott Protestant shopkeepers, argued that "no Salvation [existed] out of the Catholic Church," and prophesied "the fall of the British Empire."[37] Toward the end of 1824 rumors circulated in a pamphlet entitled *Pastorini's Prophecies* that a Catholic massacre of Protestants would take place during Christmas week; the appointed time passed with no holy bloodbath, but the scare had been substantial.[38] Despite the heated rhetoric, the Catholic Association urged its followers to keep the peace. In the words of one observer, violence could only mean "knocking their heads against the wall . . . [and] nothing could be the consequence of that but the discomfiture they had always had." In Connaught the priests promised the peasantry "that if they were quiet and would follow their leaders . . . , they would lead them to liberty," and, further, "to the recovery of those lands that were taken from you formerly by soldiers and marauders."[39]

By the late 1820s an uneasy and unaccustomed peace settled over Ireland. Traditional violence, whether in the form of immemorial brawling at fairs or Whiteboy retributions, had become a rarity. Levels of reported crime held stable, despite the spread of the efficient new police force; one key felony, that of riotous assembly and going armed by night, dramatically declined.[40] "A great alteration has taken place," Denis Browne, a Protestant who favored Emancipation, observed of his native Connaught. "I never knew more tranquillity than exists there; at the same time . . . there is a sort of violent agitation of mind that I never saw equalled in that country; that I think a great deal more dangerous than any night walking, or any of that folly and nonsense that went under the name of ribbonmen and whiteboys, &c. &c. . . . The whole body of the population are joined heart and hand with this Catholic Association." The chief secretary, Lord Francis Leveson Gower, described instances of resistance to tithe and rent collection as "isolated cases" which "have little to do with the political excitement of the country. I need not say what that is."[41]

The peaceful strength of O'Connell's movement first prevailed in the 1826 general elections. The Catholic forty-shilling freeholders, in open revolt against their Protestant landlords, elected Catholic candidates in four counties who, because of their religion, could not take their seats in the House of Commons. Two years later, O'Connell brought the dilemma to a final crisis when he personally contested and captured a seat for county Clare.[42] The moment was one of pure triumph. Using constitutional means, by exercising their right of franchise, the Irish Catholics had elected their leader—the "Emancipator," the "uncrowned King of Ireland"—to a seat from which he was legally barred. The crowd at the polls at Ennis was orderly, but many thoughtful observers wondered: How long could forty thousand people remain quiet?

On a dozen occasions in 1828 and 1829, Irish peasants numbering in the tens of thousands marched impressively for Catholic Emancipation.[43] O'Connell had no plans for a violent revolution. In the words of a perceptive government official, he wanted to "keep up irritation and hostility to the highest possible pitch short of actual violence and to hope by intimidation to carry every thing he looks for." Chief Secretary Leveson Gower recorded his frustration with "the novelty of [popular] meetings unattended with violence and not enlivened by intoxication." The lord lieutenant, the Marquess of Anglesey, implored, "Where is the Man who can tell me *how* to suppress It? . . . [The Catholics] will carry their Cause . . . without coming to blows. I believe their success inevitable, that no power under Heaven can arrest its progress."[44] Puzzled and helpless, the constabulary held back from any collision with the people. They stayed in their barracks to avoid provocation or moved incognito, sometimes "in coloured clothes mixed with the Crowd." But their reports were always the same: no plots, no crime, "no breach of the peace . . . in this immense multitude." A contemporary noted that the authorities "feel their weakness [and] know the slippery ground they stand on."[45]

Despite O'Connell's caution, there remained the possibility of spontaneous combustion among his followers. The government forces of order were prepared. The Yeomanry, though little used since 1824, still numbered 30,000 impatient Protestant Loyalists. The constabulary was armed and contained nearly 6,000 men.[46] Perhaps most importantly, officials at Dublin Castle had made certain that the police did not become substitutes for British soldiers: throughout the 1820s troop levels ranged from 19,600 to 21,400 men. In 1829 the numbers were nearer the latter figure. And across the Irish Sea, in late 1828, English reinforcements in the form of six infantry and two cavalry regiments assembled at Liverpool, Bristol, and Glasgow, ready for immediate embarkation to Ireland.[47]

They were never used. The Irish masses had pushed the British government to the edge of the cliff: concession or a resort to force. There is little doubt that the balance of power, over the long run, favored London; yet it seemed equally clear, in Leveson Gower's words, that "civil war would have been inevitable and interminable."[48] The government decided to concede, but the concession contained a catch. Catholics could sit in Parliament at the price of abolishing the forty-shilling franchise. O'Connell protested and predicted violence, but to no avail. Each side claimed victory. The peasantry talked of their strength in gaining "Emancipation," while the government, by raising the qualification to £10, reduced the electorate from 100,000 to 16,500.[49] This legislated O'Connell's constituency out of existence.

After Emancipation, what? Basically, there were two opinions. One was that the island would become tranquil, religious wounds would heal, and British capital would flow into Ireland—in short, that discontent would end.[50]

The more prevalent view was that turbulence in the island was only beginning. "The inevitable consequence" of Emancipation, predicted Sir William Gregory, under-secretary at the Castle, is "the downfall of the Protestant Establishment in Ireland." Protestants will lose their property and political influence and in time will be forced to emigrate. Catholic members of Parliament, he warned, will be responsible to a democratic and Catholic electorate whose desires will war against English interests. "The demagogues will now be able to boast that they have verified their own predictions and . . . have extorted their demands from the fears of England. . . . These are gloomy views and will be ridiculed by those Enlightened men who . . . laud Catholic loyalty and the disinterested disposition of the . . . Priesthood." Others shared the under-secretary's bleak perceptions. Inspector-General of Police George Warburton believed the peasantry would now go after Church of Ireland properties and "forfeited lands," for these issues "would equally unite [the people] in a common object, as the question of emancipation does now." John Godley, a resident magistrate in county Leitrim for almost fifteen years, noted that Emancipation was "often hold out to be a panacea," yet it failed to touch the deep-seated grievances connected with the land system and ignored the sectarian fervor of Protestant and Catholic believers.[51]

It did not take long for the Irish peasant to realize that Emancipation for him was not "a panacea" but a bogus issue. He would never sit in Parliament, and to gain that "right" he had lost his vote. The wretched potato crops between 1829 and 1832 made the return to the reality of rent and tithe payments an especially disillusioning experience. Because it involved both religion and the land, the tithe question was "most fearful and appalling . . . produced by real grievance and suffering."[52]

Popular protest in the period 1830–1833, known as the "Tithe War," owed much to the example of the Emancipation campaign. The peasantry adopted tactics of ostracism and nonviolent resistance to tithe payment. They were so successful that by the end of 1833 agents of the Church could collect only £12,000, with more than £820,000 owed in arrears.[53] Peasant aims were singleminded: the Castle under-secretary commented that "rents were never better paid."[54] Catholic priests, active earlier in the Emancipation movement, now played a leading part in organizing resistance to tithe. There were also reports that "Some of the Gentry of the Middle Class of the Catholics have decidedly encouraged the Peasantry in this resistance to Tithes."[55]

If the alliance of middle- and lower-class Catholics and the leadership of the priests were legacies from the Association days, abstention from violence demonstrated the marginal Whiteboy influence. The cockpit of the Tithe War was Leinster, a moderate and "civilized" province, compared to Munster and Connaught, traditional centers of Whiteboyism. In county Kilkenny, where "the Whitefoot System never made very great progress," a military officer noted that, on the subject of "enforcement of Tythe, the moment any thing bordering on that, comes to be acted on—the Population of Every Grade appears as one man in determined Opposition & hostility to the System." The most famous propagandist for tithe resistance, Bishop James Doyle, preached against the "illegal" and "barbarous" Whiteboy system at the same time that he advocated civil disobedience against the Church of Ireland. O'Connell himself opposed what he called, somewhat patronizingly, the "driftless acts of outrage" of the agrarian secret societies.[56] Numerous observers agreed that the aims and tactics of the tithe resistance movement differed from those of the Whiteboys, who clung to violence and directed their energies against the renting of land and hiring of laborers.[57]

The term *Tithe War* was misleading because the peasantry merely withheld payment to the Church; the violence which did take place stemmed from the authorities' decision to enforce payment. The relative quiet of the countryside in the 1820s was the product not only of the national obsession with the "panacea" of Emancipation, but also of official Dublin Castle policy which had sought to curtail police and military assistance in the collection of rent and tithe. As early as 1823, the government discouraged the use of the constabulary for collecting tithe or seizing peasant goods for nonpayment. As late at 1829, Castle directives were adamant in refusing local requests for police aid.[58]

The arrival of Edward Stanley as chief secretary in 1830 meant changes in official policy. He was a man of "strong *Church* prejudices —he has the *ton prononcé*," Lord Lieutenant Anglesey remarked. The people "do not like Stanley. He is too high and rough with them."[59] Stanley insisted on strict enforcement of peasant debts to the Church of Ireland. He ruled that police should assist tithe proctors on "mere apprehension" of danger, rather than actual physical resistance to collection. "Every practicable protection is to be afforded to the Process Servers," the Castle now instructed the police magistrates.[60] If the new tithe policy was heartily welcomed by Protestant creditors, reactions among the constabulary were less enthusiastic. The police were scattered in parties of five or six, in lonely outposts, each detachment being "not more than adequate to defend themselves and their Barracks." One veteran officer succinctly observed, "The less the Constabulary are employed or brought into collision with the people on the subject of Tithes, the better."[61]

Greater use of the police inevitably worsened relations with the peasantry. The revival of violence led the newly seated member for county Clare, Daniel O'Connell, to ask Parliament to provide a list of the number of persons killed and wounded in "constabulary affrays" in Ireland.[62] By the end of 1831 records were produced for clashes dating back to 1824, which, when added to later returns printed in 1846, show that a total of 156 peasants and 44 policemen were killed between 1824 and 1844.[63] One-third (66) of all deaths occurred between 1830 and 1832; in those three years one-third of the deaths came in tithe disorders. By contrast, over the whole period 1824–1844, only 15 percent of all deaths occurred during tithe affrays. Stanley's change in tithe policy lies behind this difference in casualty rates.

Whenever magistrates and police attempted to collect tithe or seize property for nonpayment, the resulting violence usually concentrated on the peasantry. On the eve of O'Connell's parliamentary inquiry in 1830, sixteen peasants and one policeman had been killed in riotous situations over the last three years. In 1830–1832, leaving aside one sensational incident, twenty-seven peasants were killed to two policemen, of whom seven peasants and one policeman died in tithe affrays.

The exceptional incident, which occurred at Carrickshock, county Kilkenny, on December 14, 1831, went far toward evening the dread balance sheet. "The most calamitous occurrence connected with the collection of tithes in which the constabulary were ever engaged" began as a routine expedition.[64] A party of thirty-eight police, under Chief Constable James Gibbons, had been ordered to protect a Mr. Butler, tithe agent for the Reverend Hans Hamilton whom Lord Lieutenant Anglesey later described as "a hard and imprudent man." The first two days passed without incident, as the group marched around western Kilkenny near the Tipperary border. On the third day, at Kilnemagany, church bells pealed for a funeral as the party entered the village. Only later did the police realize that the bells had been tolling their own deaths.

Outside the village, near a ravine named Carrickshock, the police first saw the crowd of about one thousand. Armed with turf spades, stable forks, scythes, bludgeons, and axes, and led by a man dressed in a military cap and jaunty red sash—a man later identified as "a Schoolmaster . . . of the name of Keane"—the peasants demanded that Gibbons surrender the tithe proctor. To judge by the yells from the crowd, Butler was indeed an unpopular figure: "Sheepstealer . . . dirty butcher . . . Blackguard . . . you will not have the Police with you always." According to one witness, Butler rejoined several times, "I am better reared than any of you."

The crowd showed little hostility to the police. Their leader, who had for the past year led local resistance to tithe payment, told Gibbons, "There won't be one of your men injured, nor a hair of your head touched." From the crowd shouts came: "If you give up the process-server [Butler], nothing will be done to you. . . . Police, we don't want to hurt you, but the process-server we will kill." The constables knew many in the crowd; some even shook hands with several persons. Only one policeman, Paddy Walsh, a local boy, was threatened; as Walsh later testified, "They said I was a Turn-coat."

Chief Constable Gibbons, a man of honor, refused the ransom, though, as Inspector-General Sir John Harvey commented later, he must have seen "that his life would be the forfeit." All the while, the police party continued marching until it found itself, against all military rules, at the base of a narrow ravine. At this spot a man in the crowd, crying "This is the man we want," darted into the file of constables and seized Butler. The assailant was at once shot dead by Subconstable Andrew Sheane. Chaos ensued. Stones, "flying thick as hail," darkened the sky and the police were able to fire only twenty shots before it was all over. "In a few minutes only," thirteen police were dead and fourteen wounded. Butler died of his wounds the next day. The peasants lost two men and officially had one injured, though Harvey said later that "as many as 50 or 60 were probably wounded."[65]

Carrickshock was the most lethal battle involving the police, but there were many other skirmishes. In June 1831 a detachment of Yeomanry rescued a party of police against the wishes of its chief constable, who "begged [them] to withdraw from the scene"; when the peasantry continued to resist the seizure of three heifers for nonpayment of tithe, the Yeomanry opened fire and killed seventeen people in the crowd. Tragedies like this continued until the last battle of the war in December 1834, when soldiers of the 29th Regiment killed twelve peasants resisting tithe collection.[66]

Hostilities ended because the government, even more than the peasantry, was exhausted. A new chief secretary, Edward Littleton, representing his own views and those of the London government, announced the end of forced collection of tithe and of police assistance. The new policy permitted tithe owners to collect the tithe due them from a specially created government fund which contained one million pounds sterling. The Million Fund kept the tithe owners happy, and, with the peasantry no longer paying, peace returned to the island.[67] In October 1834, Littleton remarked that it was "more quiet than it has been for several years"; he attributed the new orderliness to "the Act passed for the relief of tithe owners, and the very general suspension of Tithe proceedings."[68] For several years, however, there was no statutory reform of tithe. Finally, in 1838, Parliament reduced the tithe charge by 25 percent and transferred payment from the tenant to the landlord.[69] In many cases, rents rose to offset the landowner's new expense, but the government had eliminated the hated tithe proctor.

The Irish peasantry had clearly won a victory by forcing the government to admit its failure as a collection agency and to assume the payment of tithe arrears. If the tithe resistance enjoyed a success similar to O'Connell's Emancipation campaign, the victory was also only a partial one. Emancipation had entailed the disfranchisement of the forty-shilling freeholders; the tithe reform of 1838 became simply a rent surcharge. In any event, the two movements had managed to extort some reforms from the English government.

Daniel O'Connell, though opposed to the tithe system, had not become a national leader in the campaign of tithe resistance. His reluctance to participate in the Tithe War stemmed from his respect for property rights and his fear of alienating the Whigs, his new allies in Parliament. From 1834 to 1840 the Whigs opened important government offices to Catholics, suppressed the ultra-Protestant Yeomanry and Orange Lodges, reformed the tithe system, initiated poor relief, and purified local government corporations. But problems remained. Catholic officeholders sensed they were an isolated minority within the seats of power. Tithe had become a matter of rent payment. Poor relief reached only a few in a nation afflicted with poverty and did not touch the cause of Irish misery, which was massive and continuous unemployment. Local government reforms curtailed corruption but also reduced the number of voters and the authority of the town governments.[70] When elected lord mayor of Dublin in 1841, O'Connell found himself with little power and a narrow constituency. Catholic disillusionment with the English government was great when the Whigs were replaced in office in 1841 by a more traditional enemy, the Tories, led by Sir Robert Peel.

O'Connell had concluded that the Union of Britain and Ireland in 1801 was a failure and that Irishmen must govern their own country. The campaign for the Repeal of the Union would be the third, and the last, great popular movement in Ireland before midcentury. O'Connell's philosophy had changed little from the era of Emancipation: "Every change of political institutions should be effected by ex-

clusively moral and peaceful means. . . . No amelioration, however in
its nature valuable, in the laws or government, should be purchased
by any one crime or sin of ever so small a degree—and, above all, is
not worth the purchase by the loss of one single life." As he explained
his beliefs to a friend, "The Irish people are conscious . . . that safety,
as well as strength, consists in continued pacific exertion; and they
know that success must result from both strength and safety." The
1798 rebellion had failed disastrously; it was also inherently wrong.
The Emancipation campaign, on the other hand, had demonstrated
the achievement of a moral idea through "strength and safety."[71]

"Multitudinous public sentiment . . . could alone obtain success.
. . . The efficacy of our struggle ought, in constitutional reasoning, to
depend on the numbers of those convinced of the necessity . . . [for
the] repeal" of the act of Union. O'Connell reasoned as follows:

*Ministers are more or less affected by the opinions of the mass of the*
*people for whom all Governments are instituted. . . . A meeting tri-*
*fling and contemptible in numbers will pass unobjected to and will*
*produce no effect. Try it by this test: suppose . . . twelve gentlemen*
*. . . hold a meeting; let your arguments be the most convincing, your*
*facts incontrovertible . . . , still your meeting would be treated with*
*contempt by the Press, and your observations would produce no effect*
*Suppose 1,200 men meet to express their opinions, the reporters will*
*flock to hear them, the speeches will be reported, and the arguments*
*will reach the public; their resolutions will find their way to the min-*
*ister of the day; he begins to see what is the bearing of the public*
*mind on the particular question, his slow and immovable nature is*
*stirred up. Suppose, instead of 1,200 that 12,000 persons meet, what*
*is the result?*[72]

In the 1820s, tens of thousands of peasants had turned out; in 1843,
the "Repeal Year," as O'Connell called it, literally hundreds of thousands assembled. From March through October, O'Connell addressed
eighteen meetings ranging in size from 30,000 to 500,000—aptly
called "monster meetings." In May, 100,000 persons heard him at
Mullingar and Longford and half a million at Cork; in June, 300,000
turned out at Kilkenny and Mallow; in July, 150,000 at Tullamore
and 200,000 at Tuam; in August, 200,000 at Tara; in September,

150,000 gathered at Loughrea and Clifden and Lismore; in October, 250,000 assembled at Mullaghmast.[73] For eight months, he roused literally millions of Irishmen in a grand moral crusade.

There were great similarities to the Emancipation campaign. The countryside became strangely quiet, agrarian crime subsided, and a seeming unanimity of opinion emerged.[74] "Repeal" was as vaguely understood as "Emancipation" had been. The act of Union was the alleged cause of Irish grievances, as Catholic disabilities had been twenty years before. O'Connell called for restoration of the Irish Parliament, which meant, not independence, but only legislative autonomy in domestic affairs.[75] The whole condition of Ireland before the Union now acquired a romantic glow which distorted historical reality. He did not discuss key questions, such as the Protestant-Catholic issue, the rights of property versus the claims of democracy, or the land question. By keeping Repeal a simplistic issue, O'Connell sought to prevent splits within his ranks of support.[76]

Like the definition, the tactics of Repeal were familiar. At every meeting O'Connell exhorted the people to "abstain from crime" and alcohol, and millions took the temperance pledge. He counseled them to ignore Orangemen, Tories, landlords, and the British army; to "join no Chartists, no physical-force men, no secret societies." At Kilkenny he told the multitudes, "We will grind their faces by behaving well." The Repeal crowds were quiet and good-humored, filled with "decently dressed, respectable" men, women, and children. Held on Sundays, with priests often conducting services, and temperance bands providing music, the meetings had an air of excitement and importance.[77] O'Connell's belief in moral force was made clear in his choice of meeting places: almost all were near large military barracks and railway lines.[78]

O'Connell scheduled the final protest meeting for October 8 at Clontarf, a hill outside Dublin which was within range of artillery across the harbor at Pigeon House Fort. The danger of perhaps one million persons meeting on the outskirts of the former capital at last convinced the government to act. On the seventh a proclamation banned the intended assemblage; O'Connell, grudgingly but quickly, agreed to the cancellation and, with it, the end of the Repeal campaign.[79] His acquiescence disappointed many of the peasantry, disgusted later generations of Irish revolutionaries, and has drawn the censure of some historians.[80]

The reluctance to use force demonstrated O'Connell's great dilemma. He had relied on the demonstration of a great moral argument and the implied physical threat of hundreds of thousands of Irish men and women showing their political beliefs. But if moral force carried Emancipation, by contrast a minor issue, it could not achieve Repeal. In 1829 many persons in England and even some Irish Protestants had favored Emancipation as a reasonable just measure; in 1843 these same people unanimously opposed the destruction of the Union. Prime Minister Peel called it nothing short of "dismemberment of the [British] Empire," by which England would lose "her security . . . [and] eminence . . . among the powers of Europe."[81] The Union had been forged in the dreadful furnace of the 1798 rebellion: no moral or intellectual reasoning could "repeal" such a dearly purchased political reality. Repeal required violence, but, for O'Connell, violence was unthinkable.

In the half-century since the rebellion, Dublin Castle had increased and consolidated the official forces for order. The British army in Ireland still numbered 20,000 regulars, concentrated outside Ulster and scattered across the three heavily Catholic provinces where Repeal was popular. The constabulary, numbering 5,900 at the time of Emancipation, had swollen to 8,300 men stationed at 1,300 posts throughout the island.[82] Castle control of the force had been complete since 1830, and an act of 1836 legalized this monopoly of power. Most of the police and military stayed in the background, in barracks, during the Repeal agitation, but some constables circulated "disguised in plain clothes" in order "to make observations."[83] Had there been trouble, the authorities could easily extinguish the first flames of violence. The sad truth was not that O'Connell in October 1843 had betrayed his followers by retreating from a showdown, but that his policy of constitutional protest for Repeal had from the start been hopeless.

O'Connell's concept of reform suffered from one fatal flaw. Political questions were the least of Ireland's problems. Emancipation, Repeal, and even tithe reform (essentially a political and religious issue) could not change such fundamental evils as the unproductivity of agriculture or the absence of capital, cities, and industries. In a socially and economically viable society, political reforms had meaning: in England, for instance, the achievement of free trade and suffrage reforms was important because the foundations of society were solid. But in a poor country where agriculture predominated, where wheat was grown for export and potatoes for domestic consumption by an expanding population—politics was a superfluous subject.

O'Connell had asked the Irish masses to imitate the example of English working classes whose radicalism was orderly and peaceable. The protesters, sensing the might of the state, avoided physical confrontations with troops or police; instead they developed a moral position on an issue in order to shape public opinion.[84] While O'Connell's campaigns followed the spirit of working-class agitation in England, they also demonstrated a desire to prove that the Irish were not "savages."[85] Brawling, dangerous Paddy had to show that he could act in a respectable and sober manner; O'Connell, whom the London *Times* dismissed as "a long-tailed Irish baboon," knew that political gains were impossible as long as this stereotype prevailed.[86]

If O'Connell mistakenly concentrated on political reform, the peasant societies which did concentrate on the land question offered no real solution. Indeed, they impeded change. No doubt Cromwell, absentee landlords, and English laws all contributed to the plight of Ireland. But as the problems of overpopulation and land subdivision intensified, the peasantry adamantly insisted on their right to possession of the soil. The Whiteboys aimed at guaranteeing secure tenancies and low rents, but in favoring the occupier-tenants they ignored the landless cottier class and the basic problem of subdivision. The peasants, victims of very real oppression, thus contributed to the tragedy—but in the absence of employment opportunities, who could blame them?

The solution was reversal of the process of subdivision of land. But to consolidate landownership was virtually impossible. It would mean encroaching on the property rights of many Irish Protestants and English property owners. The necessarily massive government aid could not be wrung from the pockets of British taxpayers. Compensation claims would be innumerable and complex. Most importantly, the peasantry would declare war on a national policy of eviction. Those few landlords who tried to stop subdivision by clearing their properties of small tenant farmers made little progress. "It is one of the ironies of the situation," J. C. Beckett has acutely noted, "that a careless and rack-renting landlord who allowed holdings to multiply freely was almost always more popular than a more conscientious neighbour who attempted to resist or reverse a process that could only end in disaster."[87]

The extent of the disaster was appalling. The rebellion of 1798 had claimed 30,000 peasant lives. Now, in fulfillment of the prophecy of an English clergyman writing in that same year, the terrible winnowing of population began.[88] In 1845, and again in 1846, the staple crop, the potato, failed. Parts of the country had suffered famine conditions before, especially in 1817 and 1822, but never had hunger been so widespread. The government, which for years had avoided the issues of enclosure and consolidation of landholdings as undue interference in property rights, was now slow in shipping food to the island for the same reason. Indeed, the business-as-usual policy could be seen in the continued flow of wheat from Ireland to English markets. For many of the Irish, the famine was really "the great starvation."[89]

Corpses lay everywhere—across the roads, behind hedges, in cabins, over the fields, and in ditches. "Go where you would there was the stillness of the chamber of death." Victims' mouths were stained green from eating nettles and weeds. Bodies were swollen and faces appeared hollow, gaunt, senseless. The skin of the starving people became rough and dry like parchment; shoulders were pinched; hair fell from the head; and sores developed between the fingers. In one cottage in Cork a magistrate found "six famished and ghastly skeletons to all appearances dead, huddled in a corner, their sole covering . . . a ragged horse cloth—I approached in horror, and found by a low moaning that they were alive . . . four children, a woman, and what had once been a man. . . . In a few minutes I was surrounded by at least two hundred of such phantoms."

Observers noted that people became cheerful just before they died. They would crawl into some sort of dwelling, where, seeming to recover, they would sit up and talk before falling dead. A doctor told one visitor, "If you wait a quarter of an hour, you will see that man die." In a parish in Roscommon seven skeleton bodies were found in a hedge, half eaten by dogs. "The very dogs" in Ireland were "hairless," gaunt, and starving, "the vertebrae of the back protruding like

[a] saw of bone." Newspapers carried weekly reports on "The Progress of Starvation." No one knew how many were dying. In 1847 a provincial journal commented that the holding of "more inquests is mere nonsense. The number of deaths is beyond counting."[90]

When the nightmare ended, the British government conducted an investigation which concluded that, from 1846 to 1851, 21,770 persons died from starvation.[91] This body count, however, did not include deaths from typhus, dysentery, scurvy, and famine dropsy. From all causes, the deaths totalled about one million persons, or one-eighth of the population; another million fled the island in a wave of emigration which inundated England and, especially, America.

"The Famine" was of course a turning point in the history of Ireland. It eased the problems of overpopulation and land subdivision, but at the price of a lasting bitterness in Irish feelings toward England. "Me father was starved dead; and I was starved out to America in me mother's arms," Malone mutters angrily in one of the plays by Irishman George Bernard Shaw. This new bitterness would produce important changes in the perspective of Irish agitators over the next half-century. John Mitchel, who spoke for the hardened new generation, observed:

*I had watched the progress of the slaughter of a portion of [the] people, and the pauperisation of the rest. Therefore, I had come to the conclusion that the whole system ought to be met with resistance at every point . . . to offer a passive resistance universally; but occasionally when opportunity offered, to try the steel. . . . A kind of sacred wrath took possession of a few Irishmen at this period. They could endure the horrible scene no longer, and resolved to cross the path of the British car of Conquest, though it should crush them to atoms.[92]*

Mitchel and a few others launched a rebellion in 1848 which went no further than a battle with the constabulary at the widow McCormick's farmhouse. They were convicted of treason and shipped to Australia.[93] By 1850, even as the island continued to lose population, the British army in Ireland expanded to 29,000 men and the police to 12,000.[94]

The famine, in its brief intensity, had the effect of making Daniel O'Connell's long campaigns of passive resistance to British laws appear ridiculous. Indeed, the land question did require answers before political reform could have any significance. Beginning in the 1870s, the movement for Home Rule, a revival of O'Connell's Repeal idea, was combined with peasant demands for ownership of the land. By then, Irish agriculture could no longer compete with the low prices of imported foreign grain and meat; as the landlords released their unprofitable holdings, the peasantry, land hungry to the point of irrationality, eagerly accepted them.[95] The British government hoped this transfer of lands would solve the Irish Question. In fact, peasant ownership was only a prelude to political revolution and independence after 1916.[96]

In his campaigns from Emancipation to starvation, Daniel O'Connell may be faulted for neglecting the land question and for not appreciating the limits of a moral-force policy. But a number of observations should be made in his favor. The first concerns the wisdom of hindsight. While he ignored the increasing squalor in the Irish countryside, neither O'Connell nor anyone else could know that a million persons would starve from 1845 to 1851. His perception of violence, after all, was not of future famine, but of the thirty thousand peasants killed in the 1798 rebellion. With this memory, he could not bring himself to trigger a second great bloodletting in less than half a century. Moreover, by emphasizing moral force, O'Connell sought to prove that the Irish were not "savages," that their demands should be taken seriously, and that they deserved justice. O'Connell's place in Irish history is assured. If organized violence against the might of an established state was necessary in order to win full political independence, the citizens of the new republic also had to learn the importance of discipline, orderliness, and self-improvement in the conduct of everyday affairs.

O'Connell was the first political leader in the British Isles to use, continuously and effectively, the tactics of peaceful mass protest.[97] Others followed the Irish example. In England, middle-class suffrage reformers, free-trade Manchester merchants, and Chartists and striking workers adopted the moral-force tactics which had gained Emancipation and tithe reform in Ireland.

Beyond the British Isles, the legacy of O'Connell and his peasantry is twofold. The evolution of peaceful protest in Ireland produced political ideas which for the first time included the native Catholic majority in the definition of the nation. "The mere populace," one observer complained in 1825, wanted "totally to new-model the State. . . . [Their] success would enable the democratic part of the constitution to overwhelm the aristocratic."[98] The impoverished Irish peasantry thus contributed to the currents of democratic revolution sweeping across Europe and America. And because of Ireland's semicolonial status and her racial and cultural differences from the mother country, the development of ideas of popular sovereignty holds much interest for today's new nations in search of their identities.

The second and quite different part of the legacy is the strategy of nonviolence. Again, this was part of international developments, but the Irish made a strong contribution.[99] Withholding money or labor, engaging in passive resistance, and holding mass meetings are today acceptable, even institutionalized means for expressing grievances. Political leaders and pressure groups as different as Mohandas Gandhi and Adolf Hitler, and the Ku Klux Klan and the Congress of Racial Equality, have used tactics practiced long ago by the Irish peasantry. Indeed, with the diaspora since the famine, countless Irish men and women have personally carried their political ideas and tactics to the most distant corners of the globe.

## NOTES

1. Police Magistrate G. Fitzgerald to Colonel Sir William Gosset, December 23, 1832, Home Office 100/243/252, Public Record Office, London (hereafter cited as H.O.). Transcripts of Crown-copyright records in the Public Record Office appear by permission of the Controller of H.M. Stationery Office.
2. Two excellent accounts of this uprising are Thomas Pakenham, *The Year of Liberty: The Great Irish Rebellion of 1798* (London: Hodder and Stoughton, 1969); and William Edward Hartpole Lecky, *A History of Ireland in the Eighteenth Century*, ed. L. P. Curtis, Jr. (Chicago: University of Chicago Press, 1972), pp. 353–399.
3. Pakenham, *Year of Liberty*, pp. 13, 342, 401 nn. 40–41; and Lecky, *Ireland*, ed. Curtis, p. 423. By comparison, the guillotine in France in 1793–1794 claimed 17,000 lives (R. R. Palmer, *The Age of the Democratic Revolution*, 2 vols. [Princeton: Princeton University Press, 1959–1964], 2: 125).

4. Pakenham, *Year of Liberty*, pp. 342, 349–350; and Lecky, *Ireland*, ed. Curtis, pp. 422–423.

5. See John P. Prendergast, *The Cromwellian Settlement of Ireland* (London: Longman, Green et al., 1865; 2d ed., Dublin: McGlashan & Gill, 1875); William F. T. Butler, *Confiscation in Irish History* (Dublin: Talbot Press, 1917); Robert Dunlop, *Ireland under the Commonwealth*, 2 vols. (Manchester: Manchester University Press, 1913), edited documents with a historical introduction; and T. C. Barnard, *Cromwellian Ireland: English Government and Reform in Ireland, 1649–1660* (New York: Oxford University Press, 1975).

6. Great Britain, Parliament, "Fourth Report from the Select Committee appointed to inquire into the state of Ireland," *Parliamentary Papers* (Commons), *1825*, Cmnd. 129, vol. 8, p. 696 (hereafter cited as "Fourth Report," *P.P. 1825*(129), 8:696).

7. E. Golding, "Report from the Select Committee on Outrages in Ireland," *P.P. 1852* (438), 14:81–82.

8. See J. G. Simms, *The Williamite Confiscation in Ireland, 1690–1703* (London: Faber and Faber, 1956); and Maureen Wall, *The Penal Laws, 1691–1760* (Dundalk, Ireland: Dundalgan Press, 1961).

9. William Edward Hartpole Lecky, *A History of Ireland in the Eighteenth Century*, 5 vols. (London: Longmans, 1892–1896), 1:136–170; Lecky, *Ireland*, ed. Curtis, pp. 37–52; and Memorandum on the Laws against Catholics, Papers of Henry Goulburn, Goulburn II/13, Surrey Record Office, Kingston, Surrey (hereafter cited as Goulburn Papers), cited by permission of Major-General E. H. Goulburn, DSO.

10. The three poets are quoted in Daniel Corkery, *The Hidden Ireland: A Study of Gaelic Munster in the Eighteenth Century* (Dublin: Gill and Macmillan, 1925), pp. 9, 18, 166–167.

11. Arthur Young, *A Tour in Ireland*, 2 vols. (London: T. Cadell, 1780), 2:141; and Edward Gibbon Wakefield, *An Account of Ireland, Statistical and Political*, 2 vols. (London: Longman, Hurst, and Rees, 1812), 2:617.

12. "First Report . . . into the state of Ireland," *P.P. 1825* (129), 8:36, 106; "Third Report . . . into the state of Ireland," *ibid.*, p. 298; Monaghan Police Report, 1828, "State of the Country, Series 1," 1828/2882/45, State Paper Office, Dublin Castle, Dublin.

13. Although no satisfactory economic history of eighteenth-century Ireland exists, the following accounts are helpful: George O'Brien,

*The Economic History of Ireland in the Eighteenth Century* (Dublin: Maunsel & Co., 1918); Lecky, *Ireland*, ed. Curtis, pp. 54–59; and J. C. Beckett, *The Making of Modern Ireland, 1603–1923* (London: Faber and Faber, 1969), pp. 27–28, 155–157, 168–170. For a statistical comparison, see Stanley H. Palmer, "Police and Protest in England and Ireland, 1780–1850" (Doctoral dissertation, Harvard University, 1973), "Industrialization in England and Ireland in the Early Nineteenth Century," p. 34.

*14*. J. R. McCulloch, *A Dictionary, Practical, Theoretical, and Historical of Commerce and Commercial Navigation*, 8th ed., 2 vols. (London: Longman, Brown et al., 1854), 2:1030; and Phyllis Deane and W. A. Cole, *British Economic Growth, 1688–1959*, 2d ed. (Cambridge: Cambridge University Press, 1967), pp. 7, 9.

*15*. R. Dudley Edwards and T. Desmond Williams, eds., *The Great Famine: Studies in Irish History, 1845–52* (Dublin: Browne and Nolan, 1956), p. 89; Kenneth H. Connell, *The Population of Ireland, 1750–1845* (Oxford: Clarendon Press, 1950), pp. 164, 180–183; and George R. Porter, *The Progress of the Nation*, 3 vols. (London: C. Knight & Co., 1836–1843), 1:58.

16. Lecky, *Ireland*, ed. Curtis, pp. 64–69, 87–89, 96–97, 115–121; Beckett, *Making of Modern Ireland*, pp. 167–168, 171–177, 243–245; and Sir George Cornewall Lewis, *On Local Disturbances in Ireland; and on the Irish Church Question* (London: B. Fellowes, 1836), pp. 46–93.

*17*. Lewis, *Disturbances*, pp. 3, 107–108.

*18*. Ibid., pp. 94–178.

*19*. George F. E. Rudé, *The Crowd in History: A Study of Popular Disturbances in France and England, 1730–1848* (New York: Wiley & Sons, 1964), pp. 33–46; Charles Tilly, "Collective Violence in European Perspective," in *Violence in America: Historical and Comparative Perspectives*, ed. Hugh Graham and Ted Gurr (New York: New American Library, 1969), pp. 15–20; E. P. Thompson, "The Moral Economy of the English Crowd in the Eighteenth Century," *Past and Present* 50 (February 1971): 76–136; and J. Stevenson, "Food Riots in England, 1792–1818," in *Popular Protest and Public Order: Six Studies in British History, 1790–1920*, ed. R. Quinault and J. Stevenson (New York: St. Martin's Press, 1975), pp. 33–74.

20. Lewis, *Disturbances*, pp. 179–297.

21. Lewis served on three parliamentary commissions that investigated poverty and religious questions in Ireland (*The Dictionary of National Biography*, 22 vols. [London: Oxford University Press, 1921–1922], 11:1057–1062).

22. Lewis, *Disturbances*, pp. 95–96, 99, 212.

23. Ibid., pp. 94–101.

24. Golding, "Report on Outrages," *P.P. 1852* (438), 14:80.

25. George R. Porter, *The Progress of the Nation*, 3d ed. (London: J. Murray, 1851), pp. 633–672; Joseph Fletcher, "Progress of Crime in the United Kingdom," *Journal of the Statistical Society of London* 6 (1843): 237–239; and Brian R. Mitchell, with the collaboration of Phyllis Deane, *Abstract of British Historical Statistics* (Cambridge: Cambridge University Press, 1962), pp. 5, 8. National totals for Ireland exist only from 1822; by categories of offense, from 1834. The figures understate the real level of crime because of the difficulties in obtaining information, witnesses, and convictions in Ireland.

26. Dublin Police Act, 1808, 48 Geo. III, ch. 140; Peace Preservation Act, 1814, 54 Geo. III, ch. 131; Constabulary Act, 1822, 3 Geo. IV, ch. 103. See Palmer, "Police and Protest," pp. 336–345, 460–601.

27. See G. I. T. Machin, *The Catholic Question in English Politics, 1820 to 1830* (Oxford: Clarendon Press, 1964); and James A. Reynolds, *The Catholic Emancipation Crisis in Ireland, 1823–1829* (New Haven: Yale University Press, 1954; reprint, Westport, Conn.: Greenwood Press, 1970).

28. Thomas Wyse, *Historical Sketch of the Late Catholic Association of Ireland*, 2 vols. (London: H. Colburn, 1829), 1:204–213; appendix, 2:cclxx–cclxxiii.

29. "First Report," *P.P. 1825* (129), 8:34–35.

30. "Minutes of Evidence taken before the Commons' Select Committee appointed to examine . . . Disturbances . . . in Ireland," *P.P. 1825* (20), 7:141.

31. Rev. Mortimer O'Sullivan, "Fourth Report," *P.P. 1825* (129), 8:461; Denis Browne, "First Report," ibid., p. 34; Bishop James Doyle, "Second Report . . . into the state of Ireland," ibid., p. 215; and George Warburton, "Minutes," *P.P. 1825* (20), 7:140–141. The most popular newspapers were the *Dublin Weekly Register* and *The Irishman* ("Fourth Report," *P.P. 1825* [129], 8:501–502).

32. The Earl of Sligo to Henry Goulburn, September 7, 1826, Papers

of Sir Robert Peel, British Museum Additional Manuscript 40332, f. 131, British Museum, London (hereafter cited as Peel Papers).

33. Catholic Relief Act, 1793, 33 Geo. III, ch. 21 (Irish Statutes); and Lecky, *Ireland*, 3:140–181.

34. "First Report," *P.P. 1825* (129), 8:127–128; "Second Report," ibid., p. 215.

35. William Becker, "Minutes of Evidence taken before the Lords' Select Committee appointed to examine . . . Disturbances . . . in Ireland," *P.P. 1825* (200), 7:135; and Right Rev. James Magaurin, Titular Bishop of Ardagh, "Second Report," *P.P. 1825* (129), 8:270.

36. Henry Goulburn to Robert Peel, September 13, 1826, Peel Papers, 40332 ff. 127–129.

37. "Private information communicated to Government," October 1828, Peel Papers, 40336 f. 20.

38. "Fourth Report," *P.P. 1825* (129), 8:501, 725; and Reynolds, *Catholic Emancipation*, pp. 81, 141–143.

39. Denis Browne, "First Report," *P.P. 1825* (129), 8:30.

40. Porter, *Progress*, 3d ed., p. 667. For detail of crimes, see "Criminal Commitments, Ireland, 1822–28," *P.P. 1829* (256), 22:427–436.

41. Denis Browne, "First Report," *P.P. 1825* (129), 8:28; and Lord Francis Leveson Gower to Robert Peel, October 23, 1828, Peel Papers, 40336 f. 79.

42. Reynolds, *Catholic Emancipation*, pp. 93–107, 156–160.

43. Ibid., pp. 149–155; and Peel Papers, 40335 ff. 109–110, 139–144, 218–219.

44. Henry Goulburn to Robert Peel, July 25, 1826, Peel Papers, 40332 f. 69; and the Marquess of Anglesey to Lord Francis Leveson Gower, July 2, 1828, and Lord Francis Leveson Gower to Robert Peel, September 19, 1828, ibid., 40335 ff. 18–19, 118.

45. J. Fitzgerald to Lord Francis Leveson Gower, September 22, 1828, and the Earl of Mountcashel to the Marquess of Anglesey, September 29, 1828, Peel Papers, 40335 ff. 144, 219. For the government's bewilderment with the new nonviolence, see ibid., ff. 20–21, 107–108, 118–119, 128–135, 156–157, 194–200.

46. "Dates . . . during 1818 to 1827, at which any . . . Yeomanry Corps . . . was called out for Active Service," *P.P. 1828* (273), 17: 283–287; "Official Papers, Series 2," No. 615/2, State Paper Office, Dublin Castle, Dublin; and "Police of Ireland, showing Number and

Distribution thereof, 1830 to 1832," *P.P. 1833* (518), 32:453–461.

47. Army Force Levels and Embarkation/Disembarkation Returns, Ireland, War Office 17/1100–1105, Public Record Office, London (hereafter cited as W.O.); the Marquess of Anglesey to Robert Peel, September 20, 27, 1828, and Robert Peel to the Marquess of Anglesey, September 26, 1828, Papers of the Marquess of Anglesey, D619/V/ 44, Public Record Office of Northern Ireland, Belfast (hereafter cited as Anglesey Papers); and Lord Francis Leveson Gower to Robert Peel, October 1, 1828, Peel Papers, 40336 f. 9.

48. Lord Francis Leveson Gower to Robert Peel, July 22, 1829, Peel Papers, 40337 f. 59.

49. Beckett, *Making of Modern Ireland*, pp. 303–305; Giovanni Costigan, *A History of Modern Ireland with a Sketch of Earlier Times* (New York: Western Pub. Co., 1969), pp. 149–151; P. S. O'Hegarty, *A History of Ireland under the Union, 1801–1922* (London: Methuen & Co., 1952; reprint, New York: Kraus Reprint Co., 1969), pp. 41–47; and Reynolds, *Catholic Emancipation*, pp. 161–176. Reynolds demonstrates that the traditional figure of over 200,000 for the unreformed electorate is far too high (p. 168 nn. 30–31).

50. "Second Report," *P.P. 1825* (129), 8:215, 223, 238; "Third Report," ibid., p. 299; "Fourth Report," ibid., pp. 516, 598, 716–717.

51. Sir William Gregory to Henry Goulburn, March 6, April 24, 1825, Goulburn Papers, Box C; and George Warburton and John Godley, "Fourth Report," *P.P. 1825* (129), 8:723, 843. Godley's testimony is an invaluable study of the besieged Irish Protestant mind (pp. 720–742).

52. Viscount Melbourne to the Marquess of Anglesey, April 4, 1831, Anglesey Papers, T1068/31/58–59.

53. "Tithes, Ireland (Tithe Owners Relief Fund)," *P.P. 1834* (382), 43:321–322.

54. Col. Sir William Gosset to Viscount Melbourne, June 16, 1832, H.O. 100/241/426.

55. Lord Glengall to Col. Sir William Gosset, December 29, 1831, H.O. 100/240/43.

56. Lt.-Col. Osborne to Col. Sir William Gosset, June 14, 1832, H.O. 100/241/420; and Lewis, *Disturbances*, pp. 174–176. Lewis states that, of 411 cases reported to the police in Munster in 1833, only 10 concerned payment of tithe (pp. 102–106).

57. Lewis, *Disturbances*, pp. 99–178.

58. H.O. 100/209/229; "Country Letter Book," 1827–1828, ff. 146, 175–177, 183, State Paper Office, Dublin Castle, Dublin (hereafter cited as CLB); CLB 1828, ff. 22, 41; and CLB 1828–1829, ff. 29, 41–42.

59. Marquess of Anglesey to Baron Holland, September 3, 1831, Anglesey Papers, T1068/5; and Marquess of Anglesey to Baron Holland, October 27, 1832, Papers of Edward Littleton, Baron Hatherton, D260/M/OI/1/23, Staffordshire Record Office, Stafford (hereafter cited as Hatherton Papers), cited by permission of the Right Honorable Lord Hatherton.

60. "General Private Correspondence," 1830–1831, ff. 126, 146, State Paper Office, Dublin Castle, Dublin (hereafter cited as GPC); and CLB 1832, f. 2.

61. "Police of Ireland," *P.P. 1833* (379), 32:415–450; M. Fenton to Col. Sir William Gosset, December 3, 1831, Chief Secretary's Office Registered Papers, 1831/3449 (hereafter cited as CSORP); and Police Magistrate G. Fitzgerald to Col. Sir William Gosset, December 26, 1831, CSORP 1831/3663.

62. Great Britain, Parliament, *Hansard's Parliamentary Debates*, 2d ser., 24 (1830): 390–394, 867–871 (hereafter cited as *Hansard*).

63. "Number of Persons . . . and of Constabulary Killed or Wounded in Affrays," *P.P. 1830–1831* (67), 8:403–482; and *P.P. 1846* (280), 35:237–260.

64. Robert Curtis, *The History of the Royal Irish Constabulary*, 2d ed. (Dublin: McGlashan & Gill, 1871), p. 30.

65. The above account is based on the official report and evidence, comprising seventy-six folios, submitted by Thomas Gooley [?] and Richard Greene to Col. Sir William Gosset, December 24, 1831, CSORP 1831/K25; and H.O. 100/240/4, 26. An unreliable reconstruction is in Henry R. Addison, *Recollections of an Irish Police Magistrate* (London: J. and R. Maxwell, 1883), pp. 28–43.

66. Curtis, *Royal Irish Constabulary*, pp. 29–30; and R. B. O'Brien, *Thomas Drummond, Under-Secretary in Ireland, 1835–40: His Life and Letters* (London: K. Paul, Trench & Co., 1889), pp. 82–87.

67. Hatherton Papers, D260/M/OI: 2/20, 37, 219; 3/426–430, 454–455; 6/344–345; and 106, 161–162, 1746, 1786. See also CSORP 1834/1515, 1648, 4523.

68. Edward Littleton to Earl Grey, January 5, 1834, and to J. Parkes, October 14, 1834, Hatherton Papers, D260/M/OI: 2/344 and 4/116.

69. Tithe Reform Act, 1838, 1 & 2 Vict., ch. 109.

70. Beckett, *Making of Modern Ireland*, pp. 313–323; and A. H. Graham, "The Lichfield House Compact, 1835," *Irish Historical Studies* 12 (1961): 209–225. See also Angus MacIntyre, *The Liberator: Daniel O'Connell and the Irish Party, 1830–1847* (London: H. Hamilton, 1965).

71. W. J. Fitzpatrick, ed., *Correspondence of Daniel O'Connell, the Liberator*, 2 vols. (London: J. Murray, 1888), 2:324, 436.

72. Ibid., 2:433; "The Queen against O'Connell," in *Reports of State Trials*, ed. Sir John MacDonnell, new ser., 8 vols. (London: H. M. Stationery Office, 1888–1898), 5:394–395. O'Connell was tried for sedition in 1844; his conviction was later narrowly overturned by the House of Lords.

73. MacDonnell, ed., *State Trials*, 5:110–138, 153–165, 195, 206, 266, 282, 627, 629, 632. O'Connell later claimed to have addressed forty-one monster meetings (Fitzpatrick, ed., *Correspondence*, 2:434).

74. Porter, *Progress*, 3d ed., p. 668; and "Committals (Ireland) . . . in the Year 1843," *P.P. 1844* (138), 39:183–262.

75. Fitzpatrick, ed., *Correspondence*, 2:442–448; and O'Hegarty, *Ireland under the Union*, pp. 187–207.

76. This failure to specify aims and results was a shortcoming shared with contemporary mass movements in England. See Norman McCord, *The Anti-Corn Law League, 1838–1846*, 2d ed. (London: Allen & Unwin, 1968); Mark Hovell, *The Chartist Movement*, ed. T. F. Tout, 3d ed. (New York: A. M. Kelley, 1967); Asa Briggs, ed., *Chartist Studies* (London: Macmillan and Co., 1959); and Hugh L. Beales, *The Early English Socialists* (London: H. Hamilton, 1933).

77. MacDonnell, ed., *State Trials*, 5:252, 268, 275, 296–297, 411, 613.

78. *Holbrooke's Railway and Parliamentary Map of Ireland*, Dublin, February 1846, Map Room, Lamont Library, Harvard University; and "Return from each Barrack in the United Kingdom," *P.P. 1847* (169), 36:376–405. See also F. C. Mather, "The Railways, the Electric Telegraph, and Public Order during the Chartist Period, 1837–48," *History*, new ser., 38 (1953): 40–53.

79. Lawrence J. McCaffrey, *Daniel O'Connell and the Repeal Year*

(Lexington: University of Kentucky Press, 1966), pp. 173–213. A work in larger perspective is Kevin B. Nowlan, *The Politics of Repeal: A Study in the Relations between Great Britain and Ireland, 1841–50* (London: Routledge & Kegan Paul, 1965).

80. For a summary of opinions unsympathetic to O'Connell, see Randall Clarke, "The Relations between O'Connell and the Young Irelanders," *Irish Historical Studies* 3 (1942): 18–30; Costigan, *History of Modern Ireland*, pp. 155–162; and Nicholas Mansergh, *The Irish Question, 1840–1921* (London: Unwin University Books, 1965), pp. 74, 99, 102, 226, 252, 292. Like McCaffrey and Nowlan, Michael Davitt, *The Fall of Feudalism in Ireland, or The Story of the Land League Revolution* (London: Harper & Bros., 1904), pp. 34–36, and O'Hegarty, *Ireland under the Union*, pp. 162–168, 278–286, are less critical of O'Connell's decision and political tactics.

81. *Hansard*, 3d ser., 70 (1843): 297, 302.

82. Army Force Levels, W.O. 17/1114; and Police Return, "Official Papers—Miscellaneous & Assorted," 1A/72/4/78/2, State Paper Office, Dublin Castle, Dublin.

83. Palmer, "Police and Protest," pp. 680–684, 724–745; and MacDonnell, ed., *State Trials*, 5:252, 401.

84. MacDonnell, ed., *State Trials*, 5:261–263, 271, 306–307, 395–396; F. C. Mather, *Public Order in the Age of the Chartists* (Manchester: Manchester University Press, 1959), pp. 9–28; Rudé, *Crowd in History*, pp. 88, 143, 154, 186, 255; and Tilly, "Collective Violence," pp. 23–25.

85. MacDonnell, ed., *State Trials*, 5:395. L. P. Curtis, Jr., discusses this stereotypic racial thinking in two pioneering studies: *Anglo-Saxons and Celts: A Study of Anti-Irish Prejudice in Victorian England* (Bridgeport, Conn.: Conference on British Studies, 1968), and *Apes and Angels: The Irishman in Victorian Caricature* (Newton Abbott, Devon: David and Charles, 1971).

86. Costigan, *History of Modern Ireland*, p. 157.

87. Beckett, *Making of Modern Ireland*, p. 293. A quarter of a century ago, Kenneth Connell initiated serious historical study of these problems in his *Population of Ireland*, pp. 168–183. Other useful books are T. W. Freeman, *Pre-Famine Ireland: A Study in Historical Geography* (Manchester: Manchester University Press, 1957); W. A. Maguire, *The Downshire Estates in Ireland, 1801–1845: The Manage-*

*ment of Irish Landed Estates in the Early Nineteenth Century* (Oxford: Clarendon Press, 1972); and James S. Donnelly, Jr., *The Land and the People of Nineteenth-Century Cork: The Rural Economy and the Land Question* (London: Routledge and Kegan Paul, 1975).

88. Thomas R. Malthus, *An Essay on the Principle of Population* (London: J. Johnson, 1798).

89. O'Hegarty, *Ireland under the Union*, pp. 291–329.

90. Costigan, *History of Modern Ireland*, pp. 176–179; and Terry Coleman, *Going to America* (New York: Pantheon, 1972), pp. 128–131. The best of numerous writings on the famine are R. Dudley Edwards and T. Desmond Williams, eds., *The Great Famine: Studies in Irish History, 1845–52* (Dublin: Browne and Nolan, 1956); and Cecil Woodham-Smith, *The Great Hunger: Ireland 1845–1849* (New York: Harper & Row, 1962).

91. Beckett, *Making of Modern Ireland*, p. 343.

92. G. B. Shaw, *Man and Superman* (1903), p. 150; and John Mitchel, *The Last Conquest of Ireland* (1861), pp. 201, 224. Quoted in O'-Hegarty, *Ireland under the Union*, pp. 291, 331.

93. *Annual Register* 90 (1848): chronicle, pp. 93–96; and Curtis, *Royal Irish Constabulary*, pp. 75–86.

94. Army Force Levels, W.O. 17/1116–1117; and "Constabulary (Ireland) . . . employed in each County," *P.P. 1850* (432), 51:287–290. For a distribution of constabulary stations, see the map in Sir Francis B. Head, *A Fortnight in Ireland* (London: J. Murray, 1852), frontispiece.

95. See Michael Davitt, *The Fall of Feudalism in Ireland* (London: Harper & Bros., 1904); John E. Pomfret, *The Struggle for Land in Ireland, 1800–1923* (Princeton: Princeton University Press, 1930); L. P. Curtis, Jr., *Coercion and Conciliation in Ireland, 1880–92* (Princeton: Princeton University Press, 1963); and Barbara L. Solow, *The Land Question and the Irish Economy, 1870–1903* (Cambridge: Harvard University Press, 1971).

96. See R. M. Henry, *The Evolution of Sinn Fein* (Dublin: Talbot Press, 1920); W. Alison Phillips, *The Revolution in Ireland, 1906–1923* (London: Longmans, Green and Co., 1923); Dorothy Macardle, *The Irish Republic*, 4th ed. (Dublin: Irish Press, 1951); Malachy Caulfield, *The Easter Rebellion* (New York: Holt, Rinehart and Winston, 1963); F. X. Martin, ed., *Leaders and Men of the Easter Rising:*

*Dublin 1916* (Ithaca: Cornell University Press, 1967); and Calton Younger, *Ireland's Civil War* (New York: Taplinger Pub. Co., 1968).

97. Reynolds, *Catholic Emancipation*, pp. 1–8, 175–176.

98. Rev. Henry Cooke, Moderator, Presbyterian Synod of Ulster, "Third Report," *P.P. 1825* (129), 8:365.

99. Tilly, "Collective Violence," pp. 4–42.

# Fernand Pelloutier and the Making of Revolutionary Syndicalism

*Anthony S. Baker*

## INTRODUCTION TO A TERROR

Revolutionary trade unionism became a terror in the years preceding 1914. For a decade or more, the specter haunted those of position and property as it raged from Catalonia to Lawrence, Massachusetts, to Ancona, Italy—wherever social or industrial relations seemed the rawest. It produced bitter struggle between workers and their employers, who often had police support. Revolutionary syndicalism linked anarchist direct action with trade union organization to shatter those economic and political institutions both favorable to social elites and reasonably safe from challenge by outsiders. A general strike was the means, a revolution the goal. The forces of order eventually exorcised this phantom, and revolutionary syndicalism, except in Spain, lost its punch and appeal after the outbreak of World War I. But before 1914 the terror was present in all its stark reality.

This was especially true in France where Fernand Pelloutier influenced the trade union movement during the 1890s. An apostle of direct labor action and secretary of the Fédération des Bourses du Travail, the city central union halls of France, Pelloutier was an organizational genius who molded the Bourses in his own independent image. More than anyone else he was responsible for the advocacy by the Bourses of revolutionary syndicalism.

Revolutionary trade unionism never embraced more than a small fraction of French labor. Out of 6,953,000 workers listed by the 1901 census as active in industry, scarcely 250,000 had been unionized, even according to Pelloutier's own exaggerated estimate.[1] Because the revolutionaries were a small minority of this minority, their role within the labor movement has become a subject of recent historical debate. Peter Stearns has argued that French workers ignored labor federation leaders, rejected revolution, and engaged in strikes to maintain wage levels in the face of a rising price index.[2] But the revolutionary syndicalists had urged the same tactic. Fernand Pelloutier, and after him Paul Delesalle, Victor Griffeulhes, and Emile Pouget, always insisted that labor must extract concessions from employers by direct action, both for their own value and in preparation for revolution. Edward Shorter and Charles Tilly, in turn, have asserted that French workers used strikes to pressure the government into making desired reforms. Workers, in this view, pursued an ironic revolution, seeking not destruction of the polity but favorable integration within it.[3]

Both of these interpretations demonstrate skillful study, but they are polar extremes and fail to capture all the reality of revolutionary syndicalism. In democratic societies, Jacques Julliard has noticed, silent majorities remain silent only as long as they approve the deeds of those who lead them, just as active minorities must court approval in order to keep their influence.[4] Only if ideological domination requires coercion does the link between organized minority and unorganized majority break. By 1908, the revolutionary syndicalists indeed had to use increasing force against strike breakers who came to doubt the value of so many unsuccessful walkouts.[5] Ideological coercion, however, was unnecessary in the early days of militancy under Fernand Pelloutier. Strike failures in the 1890s were less grim while the prospect of revolution seemed more real. In fact, the Bourses set the ideological tone for a working class evolving toward modernity, yet still mid-way between revolutionary ferver and collective bargaining or political pressure.[6]

The first Bourse du Travail opened at Paris in 1887 and became the model for others. The Bourses provided meeting places and offices for local labor unions. They also gave free job placement, conducted night schools, and even served as recreation centers. In most cases the Bourses were initially controlled by socialist parties and by the left-wing municipal governments which financed them.[7]

In 1892, twelve of the fourteen Bourses federated at the Congress of Saint-Etienne. This action marked a turning point in French labor history, for the Bourses soon withdrew from socialism, especially from its Marxist variety (Guesdism), which had dominated the trade union movement in the previous decade. Labor leaders began to denounce political intermediaries in the class struggle, proclaiming that true emancipation was revolutionary self-emancipation. This doctrine also engendered hostility toward the state, and it emerged at the very time France began reforms. The law of November 1892, which regulated industrial working conditions for women and children, coincided with the founding of the Federation of Bourses. But many labor leaders rejected reform under capitalism as both inadequate and pernicious. Reform by state fiat, they believed, thwarted trade union self-assertion and thus denied the worker his identity.[8]

The second critical date occurred in 1895, the year Pelloutier became secretary of the Fédération des Bourses and began his revolutionary evangelism. His work had just started, and he was still known only to anarchist intellectuals and trade union militants. More than five years later, he died in agony and poverty at the age of thirty-three, carried away by tuberculosis and overwork. In the intervening years he lived precariously, accomplishing far less than he wanted. Yet Pelloutier, a man of ability and character, won the praise and good will of all who knew him. Even the police admired him, as their dossier on him attests.[9]

After his death in March 1901, Pelloutier gradually became a legendary labor figure. Most commentary on him forms a "hagiography" sustaining his now mythical role as apostle of the general strike, founder of the Bourses du Travail, and originator of revolutionary syndicalism.[10] But he has been seriously studied only in Jacques Julliard's splendid intellectual biography.

Born at Paris in 1867, in middle-class surroundings, Pelloutier moved to Saint-Nazaire and grew up on the Atlantic coast—seldom happy, often sick, and always restive in school. Illness and restlessness dominated his life, and they reinforced what he called his voluntary exile among the workers. Tuberculosis had afflicted him from the age of eighteen. It left his face disfigured, making him unlovely, perhaps unlovable. In addition, he failed his secondary school examinations in 1885, and, since failure denied him access to the liberal professions, he entered adult life as a drifter without specific training. Only journalism remained to him as a career.

In fact, Pelloutier began his journalistic career while still in high school. He worked on the *Démocratie de l'ouest* intermittantly from 1883 to 1893 and served as editor twice: once in the summer of 1885, at the age of eighteen, and again throughout most of 1892.[11] Nor did he ever cease to be a journalist. He continued to ply the craft at Paris, beginning in 1893, after a move forced upon him by the subprefect at Saint-Nazaire, who had tired of the young man's newspaper attacks.[12] Before leaving Saint-Nazaire, Pelloutier had also editorialized in favor of the general strike. And in Paris he continued to advocate it as he shifted from socialism to syndicalism tinged with anarchy. Indeed, his lack of social position made him receptive to new ideas, an attribute that explains his skill as an organizer in a labor movement so disdainful of organization. He later admitted that his journalistic curiosity "about social psychology" had led him to syndicalism.[13]

On July 19, 1895, Fernand Pelloutier became secretary of the Fédération des Bourses du Travail, a post he had coveted and would keep until his death in 1901.[14] This election indicated the swiftness of his rise. He had been in Paris just a little over two years, yet his militancy and organizational skill had captivated the men with whom he worked and came to lead. Even the police remarked of his "intelligence" and the "great authority" he possessed within the unions and Bourses.[15]

Pelloutier's career as a labor leader exhibited three phases. First, while assistant secretary of the Fédération, he helped to purge the trade union movement of socialist influence—an effort which culminated in a permanent split between socialism and syndicalism at the International [socialist] Congress of London in July 1896. Second, he secured anarchist support in radicalizing the labor movement. But, finally, he changed his strategy after 1896 as the prospect of revolution dimmed. Pelloutier continued to stress the workers' need to organize, but now he tried to recruit members by providing labor benefit services through the Fédération: a national job-placement agency, travel assistance for men in search of work, and several unemployment insurance programs. All these services had educational as well as organizational goals. They would enlarge the workers' class consciousness and teach them to administer their own affairs. Pelloutier also adopted a wide range of trade union tactics which, from the boycott to sabotage, provided means for the working class to implement the strategy of direct labor action.[16]

Syndicalism, however, was not merely a way to change existing society. Pelloutier believed that it prefigured a future order where the Bourses and unions ran a decentralized economy without any political apparatus. The Fédération would provide the organizational core of this new society, but it would function only in a quasi-directive manner, giving information to guide the free decisions of the Bourses. The key word in this vision was *future* because Pelloutier, and the syndicalist tradition flowing from him, denied that capitalism could be reformed short of its own destruction. He believed history and economics had revealed that the proletariat would forever be exploited in a private-property economy. But he also concluded that a worse fate probably awaited the workers under centralized socialism. Collectivization of the means of production would leave industrial discipline and the wage system intact, and it would back this formidable economic power with existing bureaucratic, police, and judicial authority. The Bourses, therefore, equally opposed capitalism, socialism, and the state. They were, in Pelloutier's view, instruments of social justice to chastize the middle class and all self-styled elites, those who interposed themselves between the common worker and liberation.[17]

## THE SCIENCE OF MISFORTUNE:

## LESSONS FROM ECONOMICS AND HISTORY

Fernand Pelloutier wrote in the April 1898 edition of his trade union journal, *l'Ouvrier des deux mondes*, that the proletariat needed a "science of its misfortune," an accurate understanding of its economic and historical condition.[18] The science of misfortune revealed that capitalist society never assuaged its severity through paternalism, never tempered it with charity in order to fortify it. But, despite his pessimism, Pelloutier believed that a spirit of revolt was spreading in France. "We know men," he wrote, "who ask themselves upon awakening at what hour of the day the wind of their anger will finally blow."[19]

Pelloutier's science of misfortune had exposed a completely anarchic society. Everywhere, in this bourgeois "debacle," reigned competition and greed with their cortege of calumny and violence.[20] Capitalism had become a perpetual struggle of contradictory interests, and, in Pelloutier's opinion, the root cause of this affliction was money. Beginning in 1892, he had often denounced the evil of money, which had departed from its proper function as a medium of exchange.[21] In a well-ordered economy, he argued intuitively, both the demand for goods and the supply of money must equal the supply of goods, and, consequently, the demand to hold money as an independent asset must be zero. But what had happened under capitalism was different and pernicious. Speculators preferred to hold money in the present and to part with it only when rising interest rates promised greater returns in the future. This resulted in periodic fluctuations in the money supply which not only deflated the economy, thus fostering slow growth and unemployment, but also favored France's unenterprising capitalists, who preferred nonindustrial placements and sought government bonds or other apparently safe investments. These idle rich, in Pelloutier's view, had the security to buy cheap and sell dear, while wage earners and most consumers did not.[22] The law of supply and demand always achieved this nefarious end.

In addition to promoting maldistribution of wealth, money and the market through which it operated had spawned an entire class of productionless middlemen freed from the need or will to work. Money, in short, had divided society into a small wealthy class which lived well without personal effort and a numerous and propertyless class which experienced only misery.[23] Fearful of a revolt by the dispossessed, the wealthy perfected governmental institutions that allowed maximum freedom for themselves, while protecting and sustaining the existing order.[24] Pelloutier always believed parliamentary democracy obscured this basic reality of class antagonism. As he wrote in *Les Temps nouveaux* during September 1895, the economic struggle—the genuine conflict—was completely distorted by politics, which effaced the outlines of the social question by meaningless ideological confrontations.[25]

Pelloutier's economic analysis was obviously faulty. He had only obsolete knowledge derived from the classical economist Frédéric Bastiat, with a little dose of Karl Marx and a great deal of Pierre Joseph Proudhon. Pelloutier had never read the neo-classical economists of his own day and knew nothing of the price system. By criticizing the host of middlemen, he showed ignorance of how markets widen and incur transfer costs for the handling of goods over greater distances. But he was sensitive to a major facet of the French economy. He realized that numerous small firms, selling somewhat differentiated products, had overcrowded their respective markets and failed to achieve optimum capacity.

Pelloutier perceived this economic inefficiency, but he did so by observation and intuition not by systematic analysis. Indeed his obsession with the evil of money rendered his thinking vague and defective. After he turned from ethics to a more precise analysis in his 1894 article, "What Is the Social Question," published in *l'Art sociale*, he stumbled and recoiled before the difficulties of his task. He simply declared that market capitalism made any amelioration of poverty impossible.[26] Because he believed the Marxist fallacy that incomes were extracted by exploitation rather than earned, Pelloutier failed to realize that poverty derived from social and material backwardness; and he did not understand that, to overcome poverty, the economy had to grow and change in structure and technology.

A far better historian and journalist than economist, Pelloutier always believed that history was bifocular. It revealed that the struggle for emancipation had a distant origin, and it gave lessons relevant to the present. He understood that the working class lacked the historical memory necessary to improve on past performance. Almost alone among French labor leaders, Pelloutier knew that, to transform the workers' condition, one had to examine it in depth. Thus in collaboration with his brother, Maurice, he wrote *La Vie ouvrière en France*, a collection of articles on working hours, wages, unemployment, female and child labor, working-class conditions, and alcoholism. Pelloutier had little in common with the anti-intellectualism that afflicted French labor after his death. Yet his work was almost devoid of theory; it simply described exploitation and misery.[27]

On the other hand, Pelloutier's generalizations on falling real income contained some serious errors. As modern economic research has revealed, the French cost-of-living index—in 1900 prices—fell almost steadily from 110 in 1880 to 97 in 1905, with a bulge at 104.3 in 1894 as the Meline tariff of 1892 briefly allowed agricultural prices to shoot above the international market level. Eventually, however, demographic stagnation and income-inelastic demand for foodstuffs dampened agricultural prices and deflated the index. At the same time, average industrial wages rose from 1,200 francs in 1891 to 1,373 francs in 1906.[28] But Pelloutier's gloomy picture of working-class life still contained much truth. During the long recession to 1896, reinforced by sluggish demand within the low-income agricultural sector, many workers experienced only casual, intermittant employment.[29] And without unemployment benefits, these underemployed workers faced privation.

Although a poor theorist, Pelloutier was a good observer of fact and far too scrupulous a journalist to distort it. He discovered that underemployed workers, unable to pay rent in the newly rebuilt sections of Paris, retired to the already overcrowded east and north: to La Villette, the Goutte-d'or, and Montmartre, where in dark and sordid alleys they jostled one another in unwholesome promiscuity. Endless quarrels and cheerless fornications took place amidst the stench of sweat and excrement issuing from windowless rooms and open latrines.[30] Not surprisingly the proletariat hastened its degeneracy through alcohol. Men abandoned themselves to spirits as a form of social anesthesia, and, while consumption had risen among the entire population, its severest impact fell on the poor—bringing illness and early death. After learning of how the working class lived and died, Pelloutier believed no decent person could restain from being angry or fail to see the need for revolution.[31]

Harsh working conditions, often more than ten hours a day, victimized the French laboring class. In many industries, exhausting labor was the rule, and frequently it was accompanied with poor safety and hygiene. Pelloutier realized that some foreign industrialists had found that the eight-hour day increased output, but he discounted the chances of its introduction to France. French industrialists claimed an entrepreneural right to hire and fire; they imposed whatever conditions they wished, even a work day so long that it led to exhaustion and a drop in labor productivity.[32] Employers refused voluntarily to negotiate about their right of command within the shop, and French unions in the 1890s lacked the strength to modify this behavior. Nor did Pelloutier think that reform legislation would ever work in France. Indeed, its application might aggravate an already bad situation, because laws would completely destroy the charitable instincts of employers and their fear of public opinion. As he wrote in 1895, when "the Gospel disappears, the law code replaces it; and man no longer says: what should I do" but "what can I get away with doing?"[33]

Pelloutier's science of misfortune had revealed that capitalism could not transform itself. Because the industrial obligarchy controlled the state, the state was a reflection of capitalism and would never reform the inequalities of wealth.[34] But Pelloutier did not think that he had locked himself within a universe of inaction. He concluded that, if politics, social legislation, and partial strikes were not very effective, there remained the ultimate weapon—a revolutionary general strike. Success in the revolution, however, required working-class education that would teach the dynamics of self-emancipation. Pelloutier always stressed education within the Bourses du Travail, for they were, in his opinion, "schools of revolution, production, and self-government."[35]


## EDUCATE FOR REVOLUTION

Fernand Pelloutier was obsessed with education; he believed that all labor activity had both educational and trade union objectives. This was true of labor benefit services, union organization, and even partial strikes which had value only in the solidarity they fostered. The purpose of revolutionary education was to convince the workers they could act by themselves to force social change. Indeed, it was essential for making revolution and for creating a postrevolutionary society. Thus, without illusions, Pelloutier tried to change the workers through an education that gave them skill, dignity, and strength.[36] He never viewed the working class as bound by its social status to embrace either socialism or syndicalism, revolution or reform. It was certainly not the historical agent used by Marxist philosophy to explain social change. The workers were simply what they made of themselves. In short, society would never be changed in the absence of a change in people.[37] Pelloutier had ceased to believe in an imminent revolution after 1896, but he still claimed that the workers must be prepared to identify and exploit it for their own emancipation when it did come.

Pelloutier recognized, however, that revolutionary education was a necessity difficult to attain. In the August 1895 issue of *La Question sociale*, he wrote that the French public school system tried to defuse the class struggle by teaching those ideas best calculated to ensure support for capitalism. It successfully provided the "best instrument" of social pacification, a "safeguard for the upper classes" all the more perfect since it made less necessary any recourse to violent repression.[38] But if the public schools served well for class domination, they gave very inadequate instruction. The learn-by-rote system produced only "hybrids," as Pelloutier called them, unfit either for the professions or for manual work. Instead, he advised that education should stress problem solving, encourage the developing of personal initiative, and "exercise the mind and not the memory."[39] It must also be free from ideological interference by the state, for the sole purpose of education was to equip the young for life.

Hostility toward public education, and its rigid but inept teaching, did not originate with Pelloutier. It has been expressed earlier by Proudhon, by the First International Socialist Congress of Geneva in 1866, and by the Paris Commune in 1871.[40] Over twenty years later, during the calm before the Dreyfus Affair, even Maurice Barrès commented on education and sounded more like an anarchist than the right-wing nationalist he soon became. "Scholastic mechanization as well as industrial mechanization," Barrès wrote, "thwarts the harmonious development of the individual, the expansion of his strength and of his sociability."[41] But this prior concern for education in no way diminishes the sharpness of Pelloutier's attack on the school system as the guardian of a class society.

Pelloutier also warned that education was not alone in dispensing social anesthesia. It permeated French culture, aided by writers who served the middle class. They offered a literature of pure evasion, which induced social conformity by diverting workers from the class struggle. This literature, Pelloutier believed, played a vital ideological role, for without such drivel bourgeois society would have been swept away long ago.[42] In a public lecture he delivered in May 1896, sponsored by the Social Art study group and attended by a large audience, including the police, Pelloutier spoke at length in a rasping voice on the pathological distortion of French literature. He described its decadence and immorality, and he vilified its obsession with the exotic and extraordinary. He summarily rejected the enchantment with mysticism, occultism, theosophy, and Asian religions.[43] "Outrages to common sense," he cried, "charlatanism, eroticism, folly! These are the arms, more sure and sharper than steel, which strike the victims of the bourgeois Minotaur."[44] Indeed, this straining for the sensational had tainted much of symbolist literature in the 1890s. Pelloutier always denounced just vapid nonsense, and he contrasted it to the "healthy realism" of Emile Zola, which he said, "incites reprobation" on the part of readers.[45] But this hostility was not a question of prudish morality. Quite the contrary, for Pelloutier, who never married his mistress, was a constant troubador of free love. What he condemned was the deep narcosis that symbolism had induced in the masses, the suppression of their instinct to revolt.[46]

Pelloutier now focused on the role of revolutionary art. Artists, he proclaimed, must vent their anger at injustice; for just as "bourgeois art does more to maintain capitalism than does repressive force, so revolutionary art will do more to achieve free communism than all acts of revolt inspired by an excess of suffering."[47] Thus Pelloutier defined revolution not as a response to specific exploitations, however severe, but as something to be prepared in the minds of men. Yet he had no illusions about the capacity of French workers to respond to this appeal. Indeed, from his realistic assessment of their lack of training, sense of responsibility, or social consciousness, emerged the importance of social art in his view: to educate them for revolution.[48]

*Fernand Pelloutier · 49*

Education was also a major task of the Bourses du Travail. Pell-outier placed it second only to the unemployment benefit programs. Education took precedence over propaganda, strikes, and agitation against undesired legislation. With some exaggeration, Pelloutier even claimed that "there is not a Bourse du Travail which does not have a library."[49] The government itself shared this view, for a staff report in the Ministry of Public Instruction, on the educational role of the Bourses, stated clearly in 1898, "The Bourses are becoming the universities of the workers."[50] Much of this education was technical in nature, and the courses varied with the industrial geography of France. In the unmechanized and handicraft regions, especially the Mediterranean littoral, stress fell on the older skilled trades, on carpentry, stone masonry, and mechanics. But in the more advanced centers instruction dealt with the newest industrial technologies. The Paris Bourse, for example, taught industrial design and electricity, public accounting and commercial law, in conjunction with the Polytechnical Association.[51] In addition to new skills, the Dijon Bourse covered an entire range of labor topics, such as insurance, work accidents, child and female labor, and even personal hygiene.[52] From any point of view, education within the Bourses was rich and varied.

Pelloutier always supported this technical education, despite some criticism that it fostered middle-class attitudes, for he believed that it enhanced the professional dignity of the workers.[53] His opinion made good economic sense. Although the French economy experienced stagnation into the twentieth century, dynamic growth existed in the technologically advanced, capital-intensive sectors.[54] As a revolutionary, Pelloutier denied that wages could rise under capitalism, but he intuitively and correctly sensed they might. Indeed, competitive bidding for labor in the advanced sectors was pulling the wage structure apart in favor of those skill families—electricity, hydrolics, machine repair, and metallurgy—which were indispensable to modern industry.[55] Pelloutier, in short, was urging skills so that workers could raise their wages by the promotion effect. He always stressed that worker education had its specific aims as well as its revolutionary goals.

But Pelloutier never wanted this educational training to foster social harmony. Quite the contrary: "Let us continue working for popular instruction," he advised, "so that the social revolution, erupting once it is prepared in men's minds, will free us completely from authority and exploitation."[56] In 1898, Pelloutier tried to implement this idea when he began an ambitious but unsuccessful project for the creation of a labor museum in every Brouse du Travail. Through the study of models, samples, and graphics, he hoped that workers would learn about capitalist exploitation.[57] He also wanted to create working-class primary schools within the Bourses to supplement technical instruction. When the national congress of Bourses in 1900 approved his plan, it represented the victory of Pelloutier's view that education must develop problem solving and responsibility, not convey a "stock" of knowledge learned by memory.[58] Pelloutier's thinking had now come full circle. His revolutionary vision, in the last analysis, was a desire for the liberation of individuals within a context of class, a nurturing of what he called "the timid and fragile flower of independence."[59]

The science of misfortune had revealed that capitalism could not be reformed. Education, in turn, would instill the desire to destroy it. Pelloutier predicted, "When the people rise they will have, like fire and iron, this arm more sure than all others: moral force due to the culture of their intelligence."[60] And as for the type of revolution, he preferred the general strike. Just as education had to be a working-class responsibility, so the revolution had to be direct action by the workers themselves, an act of voluntary unemployment fatal to capitalism.

## THE REVOLUTIONARY GENERAL STRIKE

Pelloutier's interest in the general strike dates from the spring of 1892 when he abandoned his belief in politics and moved toward intellectual anarchism on account of a bitter personal experience. During this time, he served as editor of the *Démocratie de l'ouest*, at Saint-Nazaire, and participated in the city's election campaigns. He concluded that universal suffrage could never help the working class because attempts in April by a coalition of radicals and socialists to elect workers to the municipal council were met by electoral fraud. Especially frustrating was the intimidation of the few successful candidates by the "Opportunist" machine which dominated local politics. The establishment, Pelloutier discovered, would permit little tampering with political arrangements so favorable to itself.[61]

Pelloutier's disillusionment with politics, however, did not prevent him from denouncing individual acts of anarchist violence. In March 1892, he urged the suppression of this dangerous sect: "No half measures! Repression is necessary; opinion demands it, wants it terribly."[62] Pelloutier warned that terrorists who followed their apocalyptic fantasies were moral cripples, monomaniacs from beyond the margin of society. Their mad acts hampered every legitimate effort of the proletariat to improve its lot.[63] He concluded that neither the dynamite charge nor the political process could meet the needs of the workers. Pelloutier's double rejection of politics and terrorism thus produced a new affirmation, and he turned to trade unionism and the general strike to bring about a revolutionary reconstruction of society.[64]

In August 1892, Fernand Pelloutier outlined a project for the general strike in collaboration with Aristide Briand, a young attorney at Saint-Nazaire and future political leader of France.[65] This association seems shocking in the light of later developments. Indeed, the relationship between Briand and Pelloutier defies easy analysis, for greater opposites can scarcely be imagined. Pelloutier was thin, sallow, and severe, afflicted by asthma and poor eye sight, with a large head mounted on narrow shoulders. Briand, by contrast, was a handsome man who combined intellectual interests, a taste for good living, and sense of politically flexible moderation.[66] The two young men, a revolutionary and a future president of the Council of Ministers, collaborated in 1892 because they were both concerned with the plight of the French working class. But, also, Briand had been caught by a rural constable in "erotic conversation" with a banker's wife, which led to his conviction on a charge of adultery.[67] His law practice in shambles, Briand had little to lose in a venture with Fernand Pelloutier.

Briand and Pelloutier did not invent the concept of a general strike, but their work was novel because they rejected romantic social panaceas.[68] Both men viewed the general strike as a concrete, nonviolent, and legal plan of action.[69] Legality, they argued, derived from legislation passed in 1864 (legalizing strikes) and 1884 (legalizing unions), which gave the workers full title to their labor and allowed them to participate in voluntary acts of unemployment. Practical organization was another aspect of the project. The strike would be financed by the Bourses du Travail from contributions by "four million" workers and provisioned by the consumer cooperatives from stockpiled supplies. After slight reflection, the fantastic nature of this arithmetic becomes clear. Union members in 1892 were scarcely 4 percent of four million, and French workers hesitated to pay their dues then—indeed they hesitate today. Nor need one speculate on how long the government would permit these cooperatives to function, once it had learned of their purpose.[70] Pelloutier thus developed a more revolutionary version of the general strike.

During most of 1893, Pelloutier was Paris correspondent for the *Avenir social* of Dijon, and in its pages he surveyed the problem of revolution. Because the state had a monopoly on armed force, he wrote, there remained only two possible revolutionary tactics: anarchist terrorism and the general strike. He warned, however, that terrorism sacrificed the innocent and was cruel, foolish, and unproductive. This left only the general strike as a means of revolution. But Pelloutier now concluded that the strike must be limited to, and fatally cripple, the transportation and heavy industrial sectors. He had linked anarchist direct action to mass trade unionism through the general strike, and he viewed the strike as an illegal and violent attack on capitalism—the only authentic form of working-class revolution.[71] Furthermore, he made the general strike the focus of a strategy to separate the labor movement from socialism.

The origins of this effort derived from domination of the Fédération des Bourses du Travail by Pelloutier and by the militant followers of Jean Allemane, head of the Revolutionary Socialist Workers' party, the POSR. Indeed, except for Pelloutier, all the key figures on the Federal Committee—including Jean-Baptist Lavaud, Ferdinand Guérard, and Clement Beausoliel—were Allemanists, and all placed their "political" party in opposition to politics.[72] The POSR stressed working-class action and advocated the general strike along with trade union primacy. Because Allemane and his followers believed that proletarian emancipation required the destruction of capitalism and the state, they concluded that politics was divisive and would hinder working-class trade union organization.[73] The Allemanists and Pelloutier thus set out to purge socialist influence from the labor movement.

This antipolitical, antisocialist campaign had a Machiavellian twist. Pretending to seek labor unit, the Allemanist and Pelloutier used the general strike to further ideological discord, and they drove the Marxists from the trade union Congress of Nantes in September 1894.[74] The French Worker party (POF) leadership, especially the doctrinaire Jules Guesde, could never accept a tactic which undercut the tutorial role of their party.[75] Indeed, Pelloutier's post-mortem on the Congress of Nantes revealed the impact of the general strike on the French labor movement. It had produced a rupture unlike all others, he wrote, for after Nantes there existed only two authentic parties: the parliamentary party with its Guesdists, Broussists, and independent socialists and the revolutionary party of Allemanists, anarchists, and trade unionists.[76] Syndicalism and socialism were on the way to becoming separate and distinct movements.

Pelloutier crystallized his ideas on the general strike after the success at Nantes in a brochure entitled *What Is the General Strike?*. Written as a dialogue among five workers, it contained a four-part argument demonstrating the general strike's necessity by a condemnation of alternatives.[77] *What Is the General Strike?* rejected partial strikes as futile, costly, and counterproductive.[78] The brochure also condemned insurrection as foreordained to failure by the revolution in armaments, and it denounced the acquisition of power through universal suffrage, given the middle class's certain hostility if and when socialism became dangerous.[79] Finally, Pelloutier rejected the peaceful general strike as impractical. He publicly repudiated both the legalistic thesis elaborated with Briand in 1892 and their plan to create a general strike fund and to provision the revolution from stockpiles amassed by the cooperatives.[80]

Pelloutier's mature conception of the general strike envisioned a violent seizure of industry, "a revolution of everywhere and nowhere."[81] The general strike would succeed, in his opinion, by shutting down key industries and facing society with intolerable, uncompensated costs. Pelloutier instinctively knew that output losses would be greatest in the transportation subsectors, where discontinuous operation would halt steady production in other industries, making the national product vulnerable to collapse. Here was the formula for the destruction of capitalism and its political apparatus.

Pelloutier had completely modernized the revolutionary process, for the general strike was the only alternative that placed the coming rupture within the economy. The scenario for direct revolution was now written. But for Pelloutier it was not enough that the working class emancipate itself; the individual worker must do so as well. He believed that revolution, in the last analysis, had to be an alliance where the claims of both class and individual were met but always remained separate and distinct.

## PELLOUTIER AND THE BOURSES: AT THE ORIGINS OF DIRECT ACTION

After 1895, however, Pelloutier turned to a different problem and attempted to create the gigantic labor movement necessary for a general strike. He shifted from a goal to a concern with the means for achieving it.[82] As secretary of the Fédération des Bourses, Pelloutier was involved in a host of routine administrative tasks—a vast and often dull correspondence. But if the modest nature of this work appeared reformist, the substance of it was not. Even his most pedestrian acts aimed to achieve one end: "The economic and moral liberation of the proletariat."[83] Pelloutier thus transformed the Federal Committee into a permanent secretariat to direct the Fédération, and he established two national unemployment assistance programs, designed to recruit new union members by reducing economic hardship. He believed that the Federal Committee should function as a quasi-directive information clearinghouse. It would provide the necessary statistics and other reliable data to enable the workers to act by themselves.[84]

Indeed, the concept of direct action was vital to Pelloutier's revolutionary viewpoint. Direct action meant the elimination of all political intermediaries in the class struggle, for parliamentary debate always diffused social antagonism, while reform legislation lacked effectiveness.[85] He believed that a socialist "political revolution" would only exchange masters and establish a collectivized state.[86] Politics was authoritarian by nature and had no place among free people. Pelloutier insisted that syndicalism was the only "alternative," but, in denouncing authority, he never ignored the need for order.[87] He demanded both organization and discipline, because good trade union performance depended on them.[88]

In 1895, Pelloutier demonstrated his concern for organization when he wrote a manual on how to create municipal Bourses du Travail and how to link them with the national federation in order to overcome the geographic isolation of French labor. His administrative skills became apparent as the number of Bourses rose from thirty-four to eighty-one, of which sixty-five were well organized and federated.[89] At the same time, he discouraged a proliferation of weak Bourses because such "fictitious organizations" could not give expected services. Pelloutier advised the Congress of Tours, in September 1896, that the Fédération must instead require the stronger Bourses to incorporate labor unions from adjacent localities, for "two or three powerful Bourses in each department will organize the workers better than seven or eight weak ones."[90]

Pelloutier favored an ecumenical approach to trade unionism, and he excluded no one from his organizational efforts. He went beyond the unionization of industrial and white-collar labor in 1897, when he launched a campaign to organize agricultural workers, stevedores, sailors, and fishermen. He realized the antagonism between town and country could not easily be bridged, so he urged the Bourses to train propagandists who understood peasant life, especially its legendary resistance to innovation. They would not contact agrarian workers directly but would operate among tradesmen ancillary to agriculture: wheelwrights, blacksmiths, and carpenters—men who served the peasants and had their confidence. Agricultural unionism would reach the rustics as did modern technology, in stages and by starting at the margin.[91]

This organizational effort applied to men lured by the sea, who were as remote and hard to unionize as the agrarians. Nor was their plight any less severe. Sailors had long been exploited by the "marchands d'hommes"—a combination of brothels, dormitories, and restaurants—from which they were evicted to wander penniless until they could ship out, once their pay was consumed in wine and women. Fishermen also faced exploitation, for food processors and fleet owners held them in a monopsonistic bond from which escape seemed impossible. As with rural labor, Pelloutier reasoned, the seamen's distrust must be overcome by services designed to improve their lives. Fishing cooperatives would break the processors' purchasing power over the catch. Union homes for sailors, in turn, would provide cheap but wholesome food and lodging, as well as propaganda to enlarge their social awareness.[92] But it was not enough just to organize workers of whatever background. They had to be given a sense of mission, solidarity, and organizational patriotism.

Pelloutier always stressed trade union solidarity, for every action had an educational purpose. Even dangerous partial strikes fostered proletarian togetherness; whenever a major strike broke out, Pelloutier used his federal office and appealed to the Bourses for financial aid. He provided this assistance for the striking glass workers at Carmaux in 1895, for the porcelain workers of Limoges in 1896, and on many other occasions.[93] But he did not limit his promotion of solidarity to strikes. In May 1897, at a Paris Office Workers Union meeting, held to force closure of shops on Sunday and on weekday nights, he rejected timid protest by manifestoes and urged direct action through a collective refusal to purchase goods from offending stores.[94]

Direct action, labor organization, and solidarity expressed the class struggle in a trade union context. They encompassed a range of specific forms, for in addition to the general strike—and the partial strikes disliked by Pelloutier—were the boycott and industrial sabotage. The boycott and sabotage were more than weapons; they were instruments to develop initiative within the working class, ways to act directly, yet nonviolently, within the economic system. Pelloutier never viewed sabotage as blind destructive rage. It was simply a means to force recognition of the worker's professional dignity in the form of a decent wage. "We must adopt this maxim," he told the Congress of Rennes in 1898, "for bad pay, bad work."[95]

Pelloutier's major trade union efforts after 1897 involved the creation or expansion of labor benefit services. By repudiating socialism, he and other syndicalists also rejected the state as an instrument of social change. This was the context in which Pelloutier encouraged the workers to create and run their own organizations. The most basic unit was the local trade union, but individual unions were too isolated to affect general labor conditions. Hence the need for a hierarchical pansyndicalism, in which the Bourses sheltered local unions, while the Fédération grouped the Bourses and administered the national service programs.

Mutualism within the Bourses du Travail formed a pyramid of services that reflected the institutional hierarchy of the Fédération itself. Local Bourses, for example, gave free job placement and ran the Viaticum, or travel assistance for the unemployed seeking work in other areas. They also cooperated with Pelloutier's National Labor Office, a nationwide employment service established by the Fédération to control all labor markets in France. Mutual aid included sickness, accident, and unemployment insurance programs.[96] All services dealt with the frictional unemployment of an underindustrialized country in recessionary conditions. Pelloutier believed these programs were the most valuable trade union functions; they met an obvious economic need and thus constituted a "powerful means of labor recruitment."[97]

The need to establish well-organized labor institutions dominated Pelloutier's views on revolution, for he denied that capitalism could be destroyed without an effective trade union movement. His admiration for American and British labor derived solely from their ability to take successful action.[98] But neither Pelloutier nor his generation of syndicalists—including Paul Delesalle, Victor Griffuelhes, Emile Pouget, and Georges Yvetot—accepted the Anglo-American practice of negotiations and strikes as ultimate trade union objectives, or even thought them to be possible.[99] Economic performance reinforced these doubts, and it reveals a major cause of revolutionary syndicalism.

The weakness of collective bargaining stemmed from the weakness of French unions, the hostility of employers, and slow growth and delayed structural change within the economy. Slow-growing light industry had greater economic weight than heavy and dampened aggregate performance. Even during the "expansionary" 1896–1905 decade, the economy changed structurally more than it grew.[100] Family firms, moreover, dominated both the light and heavy sectors, and they avoided price competition as mutually destructive. But, within the firm, owners demanded unilateral freedom to set wages and work rules. During the long recession to 1900, wages had held up better than profits, and employers tried to lower unit costs by increasing labor productivity.[101] In doing so they encountered the hostility of skilled workers, who resented being treated as interchangeable inputs in a search for cheaper production. Furthermore, French craftsmen in the older trades could view the mechanization which had occurred and anticipate that their talents were incompatible with modern technology. Pelloutier urged them to resist all uncompensated obsolescence of skills inherent in the substitution of machines for human dexterity.[102]

Business hostility to the unions, however, did not favor resistance by negotiation. The labor movement was unable to force recognition, for, although some of the Paris skilled groups were well organized, the nascent industrial unions were weak and insignificant, if they existed at all. Many semiskilled workers saw little need for a union. Their real wages had risen by virtue of a falling price index and through some competitive bidding for labor due to sluggish release of manpower from agriculture.[103] French labor leaders concluded that they had to resist outside an industrial relations context because employers refused to bargain with unions, often fired workers who joined, and ignored the government's attempts to mediate disputes through the conciliation law of 1892.[104]

But Pelloutier's stress on revolution was not an admission of failure to create a strong labor movement. On the contrary, he advanced the general strike as a myth to inspire recruits, for he knew that revolution was the result of good organization not a substitute for it. His emphasis on strong trade unionism made Pelloutier contemptuous of the General Labor Confederation (CGT). Founded at Limoges in 1895, the CGT initially justified this contempt, and even the police reported in 1897 that it had not "rendered any service" to its constituent unions.[105] Instead of first creating local unions, the CGT tried to link skeletal nationals in an unwieldy confederation. This horrified Pelloutier, for the weak industrial federations, like the CGT they directed, might slip into reformism or become easy prey for socialist control.[106] He thus opposed the CGT almost from its creation.

A major controversy began in 1896 over a proposed merger of the Bourses and the CGT and over their respective functions within the labor movement. The Confederation, in Pelloutier's opinion, had to defend the collective interest against employers. But he assigned only transitory importance to this economic action. The Bourses du Travail, on the other hand, had to organize and educate the workers locally and prepare them for the final cataclysm.[107] The CGT leadership totally rejected this interpretation. Its secretary, A. Lagailse, wanted to reduce the Fédération des Bourses to the role of a research agency.[108] Pelloutier was outraged; he viewed the CGT as a weakling but also feared that it might surmount its weakness and become a totalitarian organization. The prospect chilled him, for he always opposed bureaucratic centralism. Successful direct action required that initiative flow up from the bottom. In 1898 the CGT Congress of Rennes finally agreed with Pelloutier, overrode its own secretary, and voted to keep both organizations apart, thus recognizing the Bourses' temporary supremacy.[109] During the years after 1898, relations between the two federations gradually mellowed. The CGT muted its hostility as it grew more confident, while Pelloutier admitted the Bourses had failed to organize much of French labor. Though Pelloutier was too ill to attend the CGT congress of 1900, a CGT delegation visited him in a symbolic healing of the wounds—a last act of respect, a final good-bye.[110]

## MARTYRDOM AND EPILOGUE

Fernand Pelloutier's last years were a "long and dolorous Calvary."[111] He was afflicted with tuberculosis which no longer responded to treatment, and it spread to the throat and lungs, causing a loss of voice and a nearly fatal hemoptysis. Léon de Seilhac, a social Catholic who disagreed ideologically with Pelloutier, described this suffering and compared it to that of the early Christian martyrs. Hemorrhages ravaged Pelloutier, but he put the resulting insomnia to use by working all night, translating articles from English or drawing up reports, always reading, writing, thinking. "I have never met," de Seilhac wrote, "such complete devotion, such courage amidst suffering so cruel."[112] Even those who rejected some of Pelloutier's views knew the value of the man.

In all respects 1899 was a crisis year for Fernand Pelloutier. Illness and misery were reinforced by a sense of failure that bordered on despair. The need to abandon his splendid trade union journal, *l'Ouvrier des deux mondes*, was an especially bitter disappointment, and the failure of the Bourses to purchase enough copies nearly destroyed his faith in the working class. He continued to urge direct labor action, to combat socialism and the welfare state, but he ceased to believe a "Gallic cock" would sound the clarion call to revolution.[113]

Despite his terminal illness and despair, Pelloutier opposed the reforms of Alexandre Millerand, the socialist minister of commerce in the Waldeck-Rousseau cabinet of 1899–1902. He denounced the labor bill of 1900 which proposed to grant legal personality to the unions. He concluded that, if labor gained this doubtful blessing, it would face not only criminal actions, but also civil suits whenever employers felt their interests had been damaged. Worse yet, in Pelloutier's view, was the Guieysse pension project. During the CGT Congress of Rennes (1898), he had expressed dismay that capitalism, "which gives the workers nothing in the prime of life, will give them pensions when they can produce no more."[114] Pelloutier's rejection of reform legislation to integrate the workers into capitalist society reflected a firm belief that an economy founded on exploitation would never end exploitation and become an authentic welfare state. The sole result of any reform would be to dilute labor's revolutionary potential.[115]

By a twist of irony, Pelloutier received help in 1899 from several famous men and, through them, from the state itself. At the request of socialist deputy Jean Jaurès, the minister of commerce appointed Pelloutier as a research analyst in the government's Labor Office.[116] This rescued him from financial want but not from accusations of venality. At the Fédération des Bourses' congress in 1900, Pelloutier had to face charges of collaboration with the capitalist state. When he left his sickbed to attend, it represented his final effort, his last conflict and ultimate triumph. His illness had devastated him, and when he rose to speak he bore the aspect of incredible suffering. Bent, thin, and grasping for breath, he could neither talk easily nor walk without help. But he defended himself with great dignity.[117] He declared he had taken the job only to pay his medical expenses. He added that he had always oriented the Fédération away from politics, toward the creation of a revolutionary labor movement armed with the tactics of direct action. And, finally, he requested that the Fédération maintain confidence in him on the basis of his past services. When this confidence was voted by standing acclamation, Fernand Pelloutier received the final homage from his comrades in the Bourses du Travail.[118]

Pelloutier died in his library, amid his books, on March 13, 1901, at the age of thirty-three. The doctor who certified that the final pulmonary convulsion was over expressed his horror at the deceased human wreckage before him. "Poor boy," he muttered, "you should have departed long before, for then you would not have suffered so."[119]

Fernand Pelloutier's life and death had been a true martyrdom. In the decades which followed his passing, commentators on the labor movement tainted him with an aura of glory as the founder of direct-action syndicalism, a process that began six months before his death when the police, who watched and admired him, recognized Pelloutier as the constant apostle of revolution.[120] But the veil of legend conceals and distorts. It must be pierced in order to reveal his achievements and shortcomings—his legacy, positive and negative.

The positive legacy derived from Pelloutier's efforts to instill responsibility within the working class, from the great faith placed in it by a very ill man, who saw in the proletariat the sole healthy component of a sick society. Fernand Pelloutier did not found the Fédération des Bourses du Travail. Nor did he directly establish a single Bourse, for he limited his role to encouragement and guidance. He believed in leadership by example, and, rather than organize the workers, he tried to teach them to organize themselves. This emphasis on direct action also applied to the operation of all labor services and to education within the Bourses. Mutual aid and education, by themselves, would neither solve the social question nor unleash the revolution, but they would provide the training and competence to do so.[121] Pelloutier was absolutely correct; the only way to have an effective labor movement was to have a responsible working class. His positive legacy is revealed in the rapid growth of the Bourses under him, growth which continued after his death. In 1908, about the time revolutionary syndicalism began to wane, there were 157 Bourses embracing over 2,000 labor unions. Between 1901 and 1908, direct action had become a mystique that attracted workers to the doctrine of self-emancipation by way of the general strike.[122] This had been the final goal of Pelloutier's efforts to promote initiative within the working class.

But the Pelloutier legacy had a negative aspect which contributed to the breakdown of revolutionary syndicalism. By condemning partial strikes, he denied the labor movement its most vital economic function, that of a labor supply monopolist defending the membership against employers. When wage talks with an employer fail, a union attempts to narrow the negotiation gap by striking. In doing so, it tries to impose costs on the firm: profits lost through halted production, uncompensated overhead which the company must still pay, and possible loss of markets to competitors if consumption of the product cannot be postponed. Pelloutier, however, believed that French labor was too weak for such prolonged tests of endurance. Although he based this gloomy assessment on fact, he reinforced it with obsolete theory and an outsider's contempt for existing society. He thus rejected a major use of direct action short of revolution—economic struggles by the workers with employers. This negative legacy reveals the basic irony of Pelloutier's career. By contributing to the trade union bias against collective bargaining, he helped turn labor from economic to political action, toward using strikes to pressure the state into caring for the workers under capitalism. Had he lived to see it, Pelloutier would have been horrified.

## NOTES

1. Jacques Julliard, *Fernand Pelloutier et les origines du syndicalisme d'action directe* (Paris: Editions du Seuil, 1971), p. 258.
2. Peter Stearns, *Revolutionary Syndicalism and French Labor* (New Brunswick, N.J.: Rutgers University Press, 1971), p. 106.
3. Edward Shorter and Charles Tilly, *Strikes in France, 1830–1968* (London: Cambridge University Press, 1974), p. 10.
4. Julliard, *Fernand Pelloutier*, pp. 258–259.
5. Shorter and Tilly, *Strikes in France*, p. 370.
6. Julliard, *Fernand Pelloutier*, p. 259.
7. Paul Delesalle, "Les Bourses du Travail," undated manuscript, Fonds Delesalle, Institut Français d'histoire sociale (hereafter cited as IFHS).
8. Ibid.
9. Archives de la Préfecture de Police, BA, 1216 (hereafter cited as APP); and Julliard, *Fernand Pelloutier*, p. 7.

*10*. Julliard, *Fernand Pelloutier*, pp. 7–10

*11*. Ibid., pp. 20–30.

*12*. Fernand Pelloutier, "Lettre ouverte au sous-Prefet de Saint-Nazaire," *La Démocratie de l'ouest*, July 31, 1892.

*13*. Fernand Pelloutier, *Histoire des Bourses du Travail* (Paris: Schleicher, 1921), p. 142.

*14*. Maurice Pelloutier, *Fernand Pelloutier, sa vie, son oeuvre* (Paris: Schleicher, 1911), p. 51.

*15*. APP, BA 1216, report of September 26, 1896.

*16*. Anthony S. Baker, "Fernand Pelloutier and the Bourses du Travail, 1892–1901" (Ph.D. dissertation, University of California at Los Angeles, 1973), pp. vi–ix.

*17*. Jean Réflec [Fernand Pelloutier], "La Cité du desert," *l'Ouvrier des deux mondes* 17 (July 1897): 262.

*18*. Fernand Pelloutier, "Le Musée du Travail," *l'Ouvrier des deux mondes* 14 (April 1898): 209.

*19*. Fernand Pelloutier, "La Débâcle," *l'Almanach de la question sociale*, 1896, p. 139.

20. Ibid., p. 138

*21*. Fernand Pelloutier, "La Morale," *La Démocratie de l'ouest*, November 27, 1892.

22. Fernand Pelloutier, *l'Organisation corporative et l'anarchie* (Paris: Bibliothèque de l'art social, 1897?), pp. 5–6.

23. Ibid., p. 11.

24. Ibid.

25. Fernand Pelloutier, "Le Suffrage," *Les Temps nouveaux*, September 28, 1895.

26. Fernand Pelloutier, "Qu'est-ce que la question sociale?" *l'Art sociale*, January 1894, pp. 331–332.

27. Julliard, *Fernand Pelloutier*, pp. 171–173.

28. Jean Marczewski, *Introduction à l'histoire quantitative* (Geneva: Librairie Droz, 1965), pp. 164–166.

29. Ibid., p. 166.

30. Fernand and Maurice Pelloutier, "Les Condition de l'existence ouvrière," *La Révue socialiste* 120 (December 1894): 660–663.

*31*. Ibid., p. 662; and Julliard, *Fernand Pelloutier*, p. 184.

32. Fernand Pelloutier, "Chimères économiques," *La Cocarde*, December 1, 1894.

33. Fernand Pelloutier, "La Loi sur les accidents du travail," *Le Monde ouvrier* 2 (February 1899): 17.

34. Fernand Pelloutier, "La Tare parlememtaire," *Le Journal du peuple*, February 20, 1899.

35. Fernand Pelloutier, "l'Action populaire," *l'Ouvrier des deux mondes* 15 (May 1898): 230.

36. Julliard, *Fernand Pelloutier*, p. 261.

37. Ibid.

38. Fernand Pelloutier, "l'Enseignement en société libertaire," *La Question sociale* 13 (August 1895): 247–248.

39. Ibid.

40. Julliard, *Fernand Pelloutier*, p. 254.

41. Maurice Barrès, "Le Problème est double," *La Cocarde*, September 8, 1894.

42. F. Pelloutier, "l'Enseignement en société libertarie," p. 246.

43. Julliard, *Fernand Pelloutier*, p. 249.

44. Fernand Pelloutier, *l'Art et la révolte* (Paris: Bibliothèque de l'art social, 1896), p. 14.

45. Ibid., p. 18.

46. Julliard, *Fernand Pelloutier*, p. 251.

47. F. Pelloutier, *l'Art et la révolte*, pp. 26–27.

48. Julliard, *Fernand Pelloutier*, p. 252.

49. F. Pelloutier, *Histoire des Bourses*, pp. 178–180.

50. Ibid., p. 178.

51. Ibid., p. 194.

52. Archives Nationales, F⁷ 13600, report of January 31, 1898 (hereafter cited as AN).

53. F. Pelloutier, *Histoire des Bourses*, pp. 196–197.

54. Marczewski, *Histoire quantitative*, pp. 164–168.

55. Ibid., p. 117.

56. F. Pelloutier, "Le Musée du Travail," p. 211.

57. Ibid., p. 212.

58. Julliard, *Fernand Pelloutier*, pp. 254–255.

59. Fernand Pelloutier, "Byzantinisme," *l'Art sociale* 6 (December 1896): 174.

60. F. Pelloutier, "Le Musée du Travail," p. 210.

61. *La Démocratie de l'ouest*, May 4, 1892.

62. Ibid., March 18, 1892.

63. Julliard, *Fernand Pelloutier*, pp. 49–50.

64. *La Démocratie de l'ouest*, March 25, 1892.

65. Ibid., August 26, 1892.

66. Georges Suarez, *Briand, sa vie, son oeuvre*, 2 vols. (Paris: Plon, 1938), 1:43–53.

67. Augustin Hamon, "Souvenirs de mon temps," manuscript, 1910, Fonds Monatte, IFHS.

68. Suarez, *Briand*, 1:109.

69. Julliard, *Fernand Pelloutier*, pp. 62–66.

70. Ibid., pp. 72–74; Suarez, *Briand*, 1:111.

71. Fernand Pelloutier, "La Semaine politique et sociale," *l'Avenir social* (Dijon), November 19, 1893.

72. Delesalle, "Les Bourses du Travail."

73. Jean Allemane, "La Marche du progrès," *Le Parti ouvrier*, May 1, 1896.

74. *6ᵉ Congrès national des syndicats de France tenu à Nantes, 17–22 septembre, 1894* (Nantes, 1894), pp. 51–65.

75. Paul Delesalle, "La Lutte pour l'independence du syndicalisme," undated manuscript, Fonds Delesalle, IFHS.

76. Fernand Pelloutier, "La Situation actuelle du socialisme," *Les Temps nouveaux*, July 6, 1895.

77. Henri Girard and Fernand Pelloutier, *Qu'est-ce que la grève générale* (Paris: Librarie Socialiste, 1895), p. 1; and Jacques Julliard, "Fernand Pelloutier," *Le Mouvement social* 75 (1971): 14–15.

78. Girard and Pelloutier, *Grève générale*, pp. 1–4.

79. Ibid., p. 6.

80. Ibid., p. 7.

81. Ibid., p. 7.

82. Julliard, *Fernand Pelloutier*, pp. 88–89.

83. Fernand Pelloutier, *Les Syndicats en France* (Paris: Librairie Ouvrière, 1897), p. 1.

84. APP, BA 1609, annex 3 to report of December 1896.

85. Paul Delesalle, "l'Action directe," undated manuscript, Fonds Delesalle, IFHS; and *l'Ouvrier des deux mondes* 1 (February 1897): 14.

86. Julliard, *Fernand Pelloutier*, p. 221.

87. Ibid., p. 222.

88. *6ᵉ Congrès de la Fédération national des Bourses du Travail tenu à Toulouse du 20 au 25 septembre, 1897* (Toulouse, 1897), p. 24; and

"7$^e$ Congrès national de la Fédération des Bourses du Travail tenu à Rennes, septembre, 1898," *l'Ouvrier des deux mondes* 20–22 (October 1898): 308.

89. Julliard, *Fernand Pelloutier*, p. 257.

90. *5$^e$ Congrès de la Fédération des Bourses du Travail, tenu à Tours, 9–12 septembre, 1896* (Tours, 1896), p. 25.

91. F. Pelloutier, *Les Syndicats*, p. 21.

92. Fernand Pelloutier to all French labor organizations, circular of September 8, 1895, Fonds Monatte, IFHS.

93. Ibid.; and *6$^e$ Congrès des Bourses à Toulouse*, pp. 76–77.

94. APP, BA 1216, reports of May 6, 1897, and December 2, 1898.

95. *10$^e$ Congrès national corporatif (4$^e$ de la Confédération Générale du Travail) tenu à Rennes du 26 septembre au 1 octobre, 1898* (Rennes, 1898), p. 168.

96. Julliard, *Fernand Pelloutier*, pp. 229–231.

97. Pelloutier, *Histoire des Bourses*, p. 144.

98. *Le Monde ouvrier* 6 (July 1899): 82.

99. Georges Lefranc, *Le Mouvement syndical sous la Troisième République* (Paris: Payot, 1967), pp. 88–97.

100. Marczewski, *Histoire quantitative*, pp. 159–166.

101. David Landes, *The Unbound Prometheus* (Cambridge: At the University Press, 1969), pp. 245, 319.

102. Ibid., pp. 306–307; and APP, BA 1216, circular of March 30, 1896, cited in police report of December 15, 1896.

103. Charles Kindleberger, *Economic Growth in France and Britain: 1851–1950* (Cambridge, Mass.: Harvard University Press, 1964), pp. 172–181.

104. Jean Lambert, *Le Patron* (Tournai: Bloud et Gay, 1969), pp. 113–120; and Shorter and Tilly, *Strikes in France*, p. 30.

105. AN, F$^7$ 13567, report of July 28, 1897.

106. Ibid.; and Julliard, *Fernand Pelloutier*, p. 145.

107. F. Pelloutier, *Histoire des Bourses*, p. 145.

108. Julliard, *Fernand Pelloutier*, p. 142.

109. Ibid., pp. 150–151.

110. Ibid., pp. 153–154.

111. M. Pelloutier, *Fernand Pelloutier*, p. 111.

112. Léon de Seilhac, *Les Congrès ouvriers, 1893–1908* (Paris: Lecoffre, 1908), p. 43.

113. Fernand Pelloutier, "Le Pays de la guerre," *Le Journal du peuple*, February 12, 1899.

114. *10ᵉ Congrès (4ᵉ de la Confédération) à Rennes*, p. 268; and Julliard, *Fernand Pelloutier*, p. 166.

115. Julliard, *Fernand Pelloutier*, p. 166.

116. De Seilhac, *Congrès ouvriers*, p. 47.

117. M. Pelloutier, *Fernand Pelloutier*, pp. 112–113.

118. *8ᵉ Congrès national de la Fédération des Bourses du Travail tenu à Paris du 5 au 8 septembre, 1900* (Paris, 1900), pp. 88–90.

119. M. Pelloutier, *Fernand Pelloutier*, p. 123.

120. AN, F⁷ 12493, report of September 12, 1900.

121. Julliard, *Fernand Pelloutier*, p. 262.

122. Ibid., p. 257.

# Milovan Djilas: The Transcendence of a Revolutionary

*Dennis Reinhartz*

*And what ye see in me ye should not wonder;—*
*That I so tortured am by blackish thoughts,*
*That things of horror heave within my mind;*
*Who on the mountain height doth take his stand,*
*Sees more than he who stays upon the plain.*
*Sometimes I see more clearly than do ye;*
*At times this bringeth joy, at times but misery:—*
—*Petar Petrović Njegoš,* The Mountain Wreath[1]

Milovan Djilas—statesman, writer, and philosopher—is one of the best known and most important leaders of the Yugoslav Revolution.

His gradual ideological metamorphosis, subsequent fall from power, and ensuing persecution by the revolution which he helped bring into being has increased his fame to the point that in many parts of the world he is as well known as Tito.

Turbulence, upheaval, and harassment were constants in Djilas's life. Born on an "unsettled afternoon" in the early spring of 1911 of Montenegrin-Serbian parentage, Djilas lived his early years in a Montenegro racked by the Balkan Wars, World War I, and the birth of Yugoslavia. When combined with the lingering aspects of the harshly independent traditional Montenegrin life style, the effect of those momentous occurrences provided the basis for Djilas's initial radicalization and acceptance of Marxism.

While attending Belgrade University, Djilas became a Communist student organizer, and in 1933 the government arrested him as an enemy of the royal dictatorship of King Alexander. Prison radicalized Djilas. There Djilas not only was tortured and exposed to suffering, but also first met and had daily contact with many influential Communists like Moša Pijade and Alexander Ranković. When released in 1936, Djilas had become a dedicated revolutionary and a fanatical Stalinist, destined along with Josip Broz (Tito), Edvard Kardelj, and Ranković to become one of the four leaders of the Yugoslav partisan struggle.

Throughout World War II and after, Djilas remained loyal to the precepts of Marxism-Leninism, but his Stalinism slowly began to wane. His personal divorce from Stalin and the Soviet Union coincided with the emergence of postwar Yugoslavia. When Djilas failed to democratize Yugoslav communism he broke with party officials who subjected him to public disgrace and imprisonment.

This second experience in prison gave Djilas time to collect and order his thoughts; his break with communism was complete. Since his last release in 1967, he has repudiated his earlier commitment to communism and moved toward democratic socialism. Djilas has always been a revolutionary, but to him communism in its multiple national forms, bureaucratically administered and enforced, has ceased to be a revolutionary movement.

Several consistent factors have influenced Djilas's intellectual growth and transformation. One of the most significant among these has been Montenegro with its mountains. Montenegro sits atop the confluence of the Dinaric Alps with the Balkan Mountains rising from the Adriatic Sea. The various chains of mountains which entwine the Balkan peninsula, more than any other geographic component, have influenced the historical development of the area. They have afforded protection, in some instances to the point of cultural isolation; they have hampered internal unification, often forcing its imposition from without; and they have limited agricultural production, thus causing chronic poverty and overpopulation. To Djilas, "the land is one of utter destitution and forlorn silence. Its billowing crags engulf all that is alive and all that human hand has built and cultivated. Every sound is dashed against the jagged rocks, and every ray of light is ground into gravel."[2]

Djilas's violent and individualistic peasant upbringing helped form both the positive and the negative traits of his character. Kinship ("the clan"), vendetta, and personal courage were all essential components of traditional Montenegrin society. In the following passage Djilas captures some of the primitive fanaticism of this society:

*Vengeance—this is a breath of life one shares from the cradle with one's fellow clansmen, in both good fortune and bad, vengeance from eternity. Vengeance was the debt we paid for the love and sacrifice our forbears and fellow clansmen bore for us. It was the defense of our honor and good name, and the guarantee of our maidens. It was our pride before others; our blood was not water that anyone could spill. It was, moreover, our pastures and springs—more beautiful than anyone else's—our family feasts and births. It was the glow in our eyes, the flame in our cheeks, the pounding in our temples, the word that turned to stone in our throats on our hearing that our blood had been shed. It was the sacred task transmitted in the hour of death to those who had just been conceived in our blood. It was centuries of manly pride and heroism, survival, a mother's milk and a sister's vow, bereaved parents and children in black, joy and songs turned into silence and wailing. It was all, all.[3]*

This social behavior was further acerbated when the Montenegro of Djilas's youth suffered terribly during the Balkan Wars, World War I, and the 1920s. Focusing on Montenegro in the first volume of his memoirs Djilas recalled that "cannon thundered through my first real remembrance. Bombs boomed and rifles cracked throughout my entire childhood, wounding every dream and destroying every picture."[4] Djilas concluded that "being what it was, my childhood held very few happy memories. There was only childhood itself, full of a luster of its own, of a growing recognition of the world and its games."[5]

The young Djilas was fascinated by the tales about the *hajdučica*, the semilegendary, anti-Turkish bandit–freedom fighters of the Balkans. Djilas's first heroes were his great-uncle Marko and others of the type who taught him that a chief obligation in life was to resist evil, with evil if necessary.[6] This fostered a tendency to deliberately put oneself in harm's way. Such a society also engendered a basic distrust of centralized government and its accompanying bureaucracy. In his later life Djilas combined the *hajduk* tradition with his partisan activity and experiences as a dissenter.

Djilas drew some of his earliest and most enduring intellectual stimulation from Bishop-Prince Petar II Petrović Njegoš (1813–1851) and the *vojvoda* Marko Miljanov Drekalović (1833–1901). Miljanov was a self-educated and principled miltiary leader and statesman who loyally served Prince Danilo II (1852–1860) but opposed the despotic rule of his successor, Prince Nikola (1860–1918). Miljanov broke with Nikola by renouncing all rank and titles in order to withdraw and turn to writing. Such literary activity was viewed by Djilas as an ethical duty, and Miljanov inspired him. Djilas frequently compared his own situation to that of Miljanov:

*Having reached the topmost summit of his times in Montenegro, he behaved as if he were there temporarily and by chance. Even when the prince [Nikola] and Marko were at their most intimate, the prince felt an aversion to Marko's curt words and frank, inexorable thinking. The chieftains who owed their positions to their loyalty to the prince, as well as many who had no aim beyond chieftainship, ground their teeth and rejected the self-willed and undisciplined vojvoda. Marko did not seem like a man who has a definite aim; in truth, he had not. He was simply a man to whom bootlicking, flattery, and the pillaging of national property under any pretext had become abominable and repellent. With him it was simply a revolt of human conscience—if such a thing exists—that is outside time and place.*[7]

Despite the importance of Milʲanov, it was Njegoš who exerted the most significant influence over Djilas. The founder of the modern Montenegrin state, Bishop Njegoš became the greatest Montenegrin writer of the Serbian language. Along with "classical" Russian literature, Njegoš's writing offered an idealistic alternative to the real world. More importantly, Njegoš provided the most meaningful incentives for Djilas's literary and political efforts. A writer of the epic Romantic stamp of Njegoš and the *guslanje*, the folk minstrels of the Balkans, Djilas exhibited strong Romantic qualities in his short stories, novels, and other literary works.[8]

Influenced by Njegoš, Djilas was a Romantic revolutionary under the sway of Kant and the ideas of Rousseau before accepting Marxism-Leninism. He excused Njegoš's antirevolutionary posture in 1848, claiming that it furthered the stabilization of Montenegro and thereby led to greater democracy and the Yugoslav Revolution. Djilas believed this was the only way to speed progress, but later he reversed himself and concluded that evil must be countered at all cost when employed toward achieving undemocratic ends, as in the case of Stalin's purges and Tito's growing totalitarianism.[9] In this sense, Djilas's whole career was torn between Marx and Lenin, on one side, and Njegos and Montenegro on the other, with the latter finally winning out.[10]

Russian literature also had a significant impact on Djilas. He revealed:

*It was classical and humanistic literature that drew me to Communism. True, it did not lead directly to Communism, but taught more humane and just relations among men. Existing society, and particularly the political movements within it, were incapable even of promising this. . . . Marxist or socialist literature of any kind did not exist at all in Berane [Montenegro] at the time, nor was it to be had. The only thing that could exert any influence, and indeed did, was great literature, particularly the Russian classics. Its influence was indirect, but more lasting. Awakening noble thoughts, it confronted the reader with the cruelties and injustices of the existing order.[11]*

The influence of Dostoevsky and Tolstoy was profound. According to Djilas, Tolstoy, more than any other writer, had the "gift" for recreating reality. Djilas was so impressed that he often wore a

Tolstoyan-type peasant shirt with a red cravat while attending the Gymnasium, and he later majored in literature at Belgrade University.

Djilas's early education contributed to his revolutionary commitment. He learned about communism at the age of seven from his godfather, a peasant Communist, and from two grammar school teachers, both of whom were Communists. His contact with Russians and the Russian Revolution started when he encountered emigres from the revolution who settled and taught in Montenegro. He soon developed a negative attitude and dismissed them as "eccentrics" and "drunkards."

Furthermore, the arguments of Archpriest Bojović, a high school teacher, made in support of Christian dogma and ethics, left their mark on Djilas. He compared Bojović's worldview to that of Dostoevsky. To substantiate the existence of God, Bojović had emphasized that proof must first be sought in humans—in human mercy and self-restraint—for the individual is all important. Djilas noted: "That was strange, for the Archpriest's arguments were designed to turn others away from Communism and every form of violence. But the desire for justice, equality, and mercy gave rise to reflection and efforts to create a world in which these would be a reality. . . . Later, I always felt within myself that I owed an unpaid Communist debt to Dostoevsky and Bojović, a debt I did not dare acknowledge even to myself."[12] Communism became for Djilas more than a desirable goal; it became the means to channel the violence of the Montenegrin tradition and to sublimate his own stormy and aggressive temperament.[13]

While involved in school, Djilas did not read Communist literature; he became a Communist without Marx or Lenin. Djilas was almost the sole architect of his own worldview, an original Communist, who put action before theory. Communist literature did not have an impact on him until he had already firmly committed himself to communism. This gave him a spiritual individualism and independence which greatly affected his rise in the Yugoslav Communist movement. His personalized outlook contained hidden schismatic elements which surfaced much later. Repeatedly confronted by a career choice between politics and literature, Djilas chose politics in 1932. Djilas understood that his feelings toward politics were weaker than those toward literature and might represent an exercise in self-delusion. But he chose politics because he thought it "self-serving to pursue a literary career in the face of the political and social situation of Yugoslavia."[14]

The condition of the world and Yugoslav society rather than abstract ideas brought about Djilas's radicalization. The staunchly anti-Communist Yugoslav monarchy, his own incarceration and prison experiences between 1933 and 1936, and the Great Depression all helped make him a confirmed Communist. Because he wanted to bring into existence a world of justice and brotherhood where individual and universal freedom flourished, Djilas concluded that the monarchial dictatorship had to be replaced by a political system that accelerated rather than stifled this development. The apparent success of the Bolshevik Revolution persuaded Djilas that a revolution was possible in Yugoslavia with the Soviet Union as its model. To Djilas the vision of a civilization without violence and populated by a new humanity was a potent inspiration.

He kept this vision while in prison. His moral determination not to implicate others, rather than blind loyalty to "the movement," saved him from breaking under torture which he finally halted by faking an attempt at suicide. His Communist beliefs were crystallized during long periods of solitary confinement.[15] He became one of the most dedicated Stalinists in the Yugoslav Communist leadership. "Like most Montenegrins, Djilas was by nature inclined to go too far. He was also apt to be carried away by his own ideas."[16]

After release from Sremska Mitrovica prison in 1936, Djilas immediately went underground to pursue his revolutionary career. He helped organize the university students in Belgrade but was forced to flee to the countryside and then to Montenegro. His first major assignment for the Party consisted of recruiting men to fight in the Spanish Civil War, eventually, some fifteen hundred Yugoslav volunteers, only about half of whom were Communists, reached Spain to join the Republican forces.

Meanwhile, Tito emerged victorious from a complex power struggle for the leadership of the Yugoslav Communist party, and he appointed the twenty-seven–year–old Djilas to the Central Committee in 1938 and to its governing Politburo a year later. Djilas sought to impart his puritanical revolutionary morality on the growing Communist movement. He discouraged "free love" among party members because it wasted precious energy and endangered the unity of the

Party and the ultimate outcome of the revolution. He also tried to coerce Yugoslav Communist writers into conforming to the Stalinist aesthetic precepts of socialist realism, but many, such as Tito's friend Miroslav Krleža, firmly resisted. In these years Djilas was a dedicated revolutionary, a Stalinist, and a close comrade of Tito.

By 1941 Djilas began to have doubts because of Stalin's purges, the winter war of 1939–40 between the Soviet Union and Finland, and continued Soviet adherence to the Nazi-Soviet pact after the Axis occupation of Yugoslavia. But Djilas dismissed these misgivings when he lost most of his family in World War II at the hands of the German and Italian invaders and their native fascist *chetnik* collaborators. To escape this grief he sought out a deeper refuge in communism and found himself "drawn closer" to Stalin. Djilas became a more devoted Stalinist who accepted the purges as necessary, and he justified the Nazi-Soviet pact with all of its ramifications.[17]

In 1943, while surrounded during the Fifth Fascist Offensive in Bosnia and Montenegro, Djilas came to question communism's universal truths and applicability.[18] He admired the tenacity of his Axis enemies who had left their homelands to fight in the Balkans for their own nationalistic beliefs. Real disenchantment set in during his diplomatic mission to the Soviet Union in the late spring of 1944. Djilas later recalled that contacts with representatives of the British Empire while en route to Moscow "certainly contributed to my realization that there did not exist a single ideal only, but that there were on our globe countless co-ordinate human systems."[19] With naïve anticipation he went to his first meeting with Stalin, but Djilas was severely shaken by this and subsequent encounters. Along the way he also had a disturbing experience while meeting with officers of Marshal I. S. Konev's command on the Second Ukranian Front, near Pruth. There he listened to Lieutenant-General F. V. Korotayev and other officers who questioned communism's ability or that of any other ideology finally to capture the minds of all people.[20] Djilas later remembered:

*It was in the Red Army, from an army commander [Korotayev], that I first heard a thought that was strange to me then, but bold: When Communism triumphs in the whole world, he concluded, wars would then acquire their final bitter character. According to Marxist theories, which the Soviet commanders knew as well as I, wars are exclu-*

*sively the product of class struggle, and because Communism would
abolish classes, the necessity for men to wage war would also vanish.
But this general, many Russian soldiers, as well as I in the worst battle in which I ever took part came to realize some further truths in
the horrors of war: that human struggles would acquire the aspect of
ultimate bitterness only when all men came to be subject to the same
social system, for the system would be untenable as such and various
sects would undertake the reckless destruction of the human race for
the sake of its greater "happiness." Among these Soviet officers,
trained in Marxism, this idea was incidental, tucked away. But I did
not forget it, nor did I regard it as being fortuitous then. Even if their
consciousness had not been penetrated by the knowledge that not
even the society which they were defending was free of profound and
antagonistic differences, still they vaguely discerned that though man
cannot live outside an ordered society and without ordered ideas, his
life is nevertheless also subject to other compelling forces.*[21]

Djilas returned from his first trip to the Soviet Union with the seeds
of doubt implanted in his intellectual make-up. He compared his position as a partisan general to the role of Njegoš (for centuries it was
the practice to have the bishops of Montenegro confirmed in their
office by the patriarchs of the Russian Orthodox church), who had
journeyed to Russia to seek "understanding and salvation," but returned disillusioned by this experience.[22]

In March 1945, Djilas accepted the appointment as minister for
Montenegro in the Yugoslav Government of National Unity. The
atrocities committed by the Soviet Red Army while aiding in the liberation and occupation of northeastern Yugoslavia increased his feeling of alienation. In the spring of 1945 on his second visit to the Soviet Union, as part of a mission headed by Tito to negotiate a mutual
assistance treaty, Djilas protested these excesses to Stalin. His accusations enraged the Soviet dictator, who responded by trying to discredit and ostracize Djilas while in Moscow. Upset at this response,
Djilas also disliked the privileged and decadent life style of Stalin and
much of the Soviet leadership. Djilas slowly came to the realization
that communism could prevail outside the USSR without Stalin.

In 1946, Djilas was promoted to minister without portfolio and he
grew increasingly critical of the counterrevolutionary tendencies de-

veloping under Soviet communism.[23] After World War II, Djilas began to understand the geopolitical basis of Russian imperialism. Its aggressive nationalistic impulses were stronger than any altruistic Marxist ideal. In fact, Russian expansionism continued under the Leninist-Stalinist application of communism because it was the product of totalitarianism and imperialism. Djilas responded by opposing the prolonged occupation of Eastern Europe.

Djilas made his third journey to Moscow in order to discuss Yugoslav-Balkan relations. After Djilas returned to Belgrade, Stalin, in an attempt to divide the Yugoslav leadership, sent a letter to Tito, charging Djilas with being the most prominent of a number of "suspect Marxists." This response only contributed to the Yugoslav-Soviet split in the winter of 1948. After the rupture in relations with the Soviet Union, Djilas and other Yugoslav intellectuals undertook a major reinvestigation of the Marxist classics to justify and clarify their position. Djilas also began reading Dostoevsky again, and he proved a most articulate spokesman at the United Nations in 1949 when he criticized Stalin and the Soviet Union. After Stalin's death Djilas referred to him as an "illusion" of the revolutionary struggle.[24]

After his fresh analysis of Marxism and Dostoevsky, Djilas made several major attempts at liberalizing Yugoslav communism. Djilas saw a centralized bureaucratically dominated one-party state as the Stalinist antithesis to the Communist ideal; Stalin represented the rule of a new class and the demise of the Russian Revolution. Collaborating with such party leaders as Kardelj and Boris Kidrić, Djilas formulated the basic idea of "self-management" through political and economic decentralization. They convinced Tito of this policy, which was implemented in the Law of June 27, 1950. Two years later, as vice-president of Yugoslavia and president of the Federal Assembly, Djilas reached the peak of his influence during the Sixth Congress (the "Djilas Congress") of the Yugoslav Communist party. At this congress, Djilas de-emphasized the role of the Party and called for its reorganization and decentralization into the League of Yugoslav Communists (SKJ). He openly criticized the tyranny of officialdom, offered the view that no structured working class was needed under Yugoslavia's self-management scheme, and recommended that his colleagues draft a party platform (completed in 1958) free of Soviet influences. But Djilas found it difficult to build on these initial gains because he soon came into conflict with Tito and the other Yugoslav leaders.

During this tumultuous period Djilas consciously compared himself to Trotsky. But Djilas differed with Trotsky on the origins, nature, and necessity of bureaucracy, a difference which outweighed any historical or ideological similarities. This became apparent early in 1953 when Djilas developed a close friendship with the left-wing British Laborite Aneurin Bevan. Bevan's concept of social democracy had a significant effect on Djilas's worldview. Djilas also was impressed by the nonviolent ideas of Mohandas Gandhi; he saw them as the only way to bring about the mobilization and participation of the masses in the Indian push for independence. Djilas greatly admired Gandhi for providing India with a viable alternative to communism.[25]

Djilas continued in his efforts to humanize Yugoslav communism in a series of highly critical articles published in the newspaper *Borba* (The struggle) and the journal *Nova Misao* (New thought).[26] He warned that abusive bureaucratization was an "internal contradiction" of the revolution. In *Borba*, on October 22, 1953, he wrote:

*Arbitrariness, undemocratic behavior, willful, facile and self-centered interpretation of what is and what is not bourgeois, destruction of still-tender forms of democracy, all deform, pervert, and undermine socialist forces and socialism, even if they do weaken the bourgeosie. When power and industry are in socialist hands, then unselfishness, intellect, love of truth, discussion and criticism, harmony of words and deeds (respect-obeying the proper laws), are more important for democratic progress than anything else, even if the struggle against the bourgeois vestiges then takes longer. These are the forms which motivate socialism and democracy; they not only lead to the disappearance of a class which ultimately was able to be only a slave and a traitor, but also to the disappearance of both capitalism and state capitalism.*[27]

Two months later he wrote another article that discussed the Stalinist terror, and he pleaded for an ideological tolerance that allowed a diversity of opinion to develop free from the threats of persecution. He concluded that a free intellectual climate was essential to assure future democratic progress.[28] On January 4, 1954, Djilas chided the Party for backsliding: "The final aim of a true communist is not, and cannot be, some kind of abstract party as such, catering exclusively to communists; it is, instead, elevating the people's socialist consciousness, educating the masses for democracy, and formulating concrete means of fighting for democracy, legality, the rights of citizens, etc."[29]

Djilas received several semiofficial warnings about his publications from colleagues in the Yugoslav leadership, but he continued his criticism. He was committed to an ideal, and, given his personality and background, he could do little else. He felt an obligation to those who had sacrificed themselves in the revolution to strive toward his conception of its ideal realization. Djilas's fight and subsequent disenchantment with Marxism never really constituted the basis for a "movement," but his critiques found a good deal of popular support.[30]

Unfortunately for Djilas, Tito felt betrayed by his younger compatriot, and he brought the case of Djilas before the extraordinary Third Plenum of the SKJ on January 17, 1954. With only his ex-wife Mitra Mitrović and the historian Vladimir Dedijer on his side, Djilas stood almost alone, and the severity of the official reaction concerned him. Near the end of the session he made a partial "recantation," which demonstrated that his break with communism was not yet final.[31] This had little impact on his comrades, who stripped Djilas of his more important state and Party offices.

After this trial Djilas entered into a period of intellectual confusion. But the ingrained strengths of his peasant character helped preserve Djilas's mental lucidity in this difficult period. He gradually came to the realization that "history is not only created by the victors, but also by vanquished visionaries." He wrote, "I am not a creator of history, I am one of the visionaries—one of the smallest and least significant ones."[32] In March 1954, he resigned from the SKJ, and he soon revoked his "recantation." He concluded that the Marxist utopia was a myth.

Djilas's position further deteriorated when Nikita Khrushchev, a "dynamic pragmatist," began to improve Yugoslav-Soviet relations.[33] Rapprochement came into full bloom with Khrushchev's visit to Yugoslavia in 1955. Djilas soon faced charges under Article 118 of the Yugoslav Criminal Code, because he had conducted propaganda hostile to the state and granted an exclusive interview to the *New York Times*. He was found guilty and given an eighteen-month suspended sentence. Djilas's situation was now directly subject to Yugoslavia's relationship with the Soviet Union, which found him offensive.

Despite this harassment, Djilas began to write again in a literary vein. His Montenegrin roots and childhood served as the inspiration and subject; *Land without Justice* was the outcome.[34] This manuscript remained unpublished because its central theme of individuals destined to strive for unattainable perfection was deemed insulting to the Soviet Union. Djilas then made the difficult and courageous decision to send his manuscripts to the West for translation and publication.[35]

The suppression of the 1956 Hungarian uprising severely threatened the new Yugoslav-Soviet rapprochement. Djilas was immediately arrested for his article "The Storm in Eastern Europe," which appeared in *U.S. News and World Report*. He identified the Hungarian revolt as a manifestation of national communism, a popular struggle against dominance from Moscow, while Yugoslavia's break with the Soviet Union in 1948 represented a rebellion of the Yugoslav leadership. Djilas indicated that Yugoslavia's democratic foundations were weaker than Hungary's, and he predicted that events in Yugoslavia and Hungary signaled the disintegration of global communism.[36] Djilas was tried again and given three years at hard labor, but just before his incarceration he managed to send the manuscript of *The New Class* abroad. Its publication led to a third trial, where the judges added four more years to his sentence.[37]

In 1961, Djilas signed an article of submission and was released.[38] He wrote of this experience: "I realized that the state leaders needed it for further blackmail, and this later proved to be the purpose, but my literary and other plans made it essential for me to get out of prison."[39] One year later he was rearrested and tried under Article 320 of the Yugoslav Criminal Code for revealing state secrets by publishing *Conversations with Stalin*. This time he received nine years in prison, but the authorities freed him after four years because of failing health.

Djilas enjoyed his freedom, but he realized that it was behind bars, where he first established his belief in Marx and Lenin, that he had formulated a new intellectual-philosophical position. Although disenchanted with communism, Djilas still valued Marx as a historical personage. Influenced by Marx's humanism, Djilas continued to oppose systems that tried to subjugate or destroy human individualism. Djilas stressed that communism, capitalism, and Christianity all needed to modify their beliefs and institutions, but "ideas are like vampires; ideas are capable of living after the death of the generations and social conditions in and by which they were inspired."[40]

In 1968, Djilas resumed writing about politics, and he generally commented about the state of the world. After the Czechoslovakian invasion, which had a profound effect on Yugoslav-Soviet relations, he was allowed to travel to Western Europe and the United States. According to Djilas, the Warsaw Pact occupation of Czechoslovakia demonstrated the degenerate nature of the Soviet bureaucracy, which had to stamp out heresies at home and abroad to prevent greater decay.[41] Djilas believed that Czechoslovakia's failure to resist deluded much of the rest of the world into thinking that this invasion was merely a struggle between Communists, rather than an act of Soviet aggression. He warned that the Soviet Union should be isolated from the rest of the world as a "moral leper."[42]

Djilas's alienation from communism was certainly not unique; Nikolai Berdayaev, Vladimir Dedijer, Mihajlo Mihajlov, and Leszek Kolakowski all have had comparable experiences. Djilas lamented that the revolution "gave me everything—except what I idealistically expected from it."[43] For Djilas, social justice remained as elusive as ever.

At present, Djilas is committed to a form of democratic socialism with its permissiveness toward human individualism as an antidote to Communist bureaucratic despotism.[44] According to Djilas: "The twilight of the ideologies does not mean an end to Utopia. They are not the same—though every ideology contains within itself something of a Utopia—for Utopias are enthusiasm and impulse in the struggle for good and for happiness of men and of nations. New Utopias will be born inspired by the cosmic potential of mankind."[45]

Literature remained an important source of inspiration for Djilas. In prison he had translated Milton into Serbo-Croatian (on toilet paper). He looked to Milton as a writer who dealt squarely with the problems of good and evil and was inspired by Milton's resolution in overcoming blindness.[46] Djilas also probed existentialism. He rejected Sartre as too formal, but Djilas was amazed by how much he had in common with Camus. Djilas found *The Myth of Sisyphus* especially enlightening because Camus had confronted the question of suicide after the fall of France in 1940, questioned the meaning of life, and speculated about the reasons for living and dying. Camus concluded that "defiiance" was man's only proven "truth": "The revolt gives life its value. Spread out over the whole length of a life, it restores its majesty to that life. To a man devoid of blinders, there is no finer sight than that of the intelligence at grips with a reality that transcends it. The sight of human pride is unequaled. No disparagement is of any use."[47] Djilas concurred with this analysis because it supported his own "existential humanism" and relativist view of historical development.[48]

Recently Djilas has become interested in Solzhenitsyn. According to Djilas, Solzhenitsyn lacked "fantasy and imagination," but when describing personal ordeals he was an excellent "artistic witness." Djilas compared Solzhenitsyn's efforts to humanize the Soviet Union to those of Dostoevsky a century earlier, but Djilas also accused Solzhenitsyn of falsely believing that Bolshevism was a historical "accident" in Russia. Djilas singled out the "Gulag Archipelago" as the greatest disgrace of communism; he berated the Soviet Union as the Communist fatherland of the concentration camps.[49]

Many of the striking actions and ideas of Djilas's career have been carried out in compliance with or in reaction to the basic dictates of his Montenegrin heritage. His roots, like those of the stalwart trees of the mountain forests, go deeper than ever into its rocky soil. Montenegro gave him life, and to that life definition and direction. It brought inner conflict and disarray but also furnished stability and a firm foundation for his existential humanism, and it provided aesthetic inspiration. With Montenegro in mind, Djilas wrote: "It is not true that one's homeland is wherever it is good. Man is born once and only once in one place. There is only one homeland."[50]

Currently, Djilas is searching his past and that of his people for future directions. In his novel *Montenegro*, Djilas speaks through the character Mališa Petrović, who makes the following observation:

*The Serb people of Montenegro are my people. I know that there are Serbs without Montenegro and that there can be no Montenegro without Serbs. But for me there can be no Serbs without Montenegro.*

*When Montenegro perishes, I perish with it. I can do without my head but I cannot do without my soul. I am fighting for what I have. . . . You are evil and accursed, Montenegro, above any country in the world; yet even as you are, you are dear to me. You have been steeped in the blackest evil and in the highest good, and they wage in you a fight that never ceases. Where will you find a man? Here. Where will you find a Serb? Here. Where will you find a renegade? Here. In you the human race is mirrored. . . . Let the song of Kossovo remain to witness: it cannot die. . . . We are small. We are weak. Worse and stronger enemies have trampled on us, but we have never given them our soul, nor have we ever surrendered the Serb Idea.*[51]

Fearlessly, Djilas is still groping for a Tolstoyan-Gandhian worldview to provide a counterreality to Montenegro. Concerning the future, he expresses the traditional Slavic pessimism, which outside the Balkans may be taken as very guarded optimism: "The future is for those who see far."[52]

## NOTES

1. Petar Petrović Njegoš, *The Mountain Wreath*, trans. James W. Wiles (London: George Allen and Unwin, 1930; reprint, Westport, Conn.: Greenwood Press, 1970), p. 99. Used with agreement of the reprint publisher, Greenwood Press, a division of Williamhouse-Regency Inc.
2. Milovan Djilas, *Njegoš: Poet, Prince, Bishop*, trans. Michael B. Petrovich (New York: Harcourt, Brace and World, 1966), p. 13.
3. Milovan Djilas, *Land without Justice*, trans. Michael B. Petrovich (New York: Harcourt Brace Jovanovich, 1958), p. 107.
4. Ibid., p. 42.
5. Ibid., p. 110.
6. Ibid., pp. 8–12.
7. Milovan Djilas, "About Marko Miljanov," in *The Stone and the Violets*, trans. Lovett F. Edwards (New York: Harcourt Brace Jovanovich, 1972), pp. 223–224; and idem, *Parts of a Lifetime*, ed. Michael and Deborah Milenkovich (New York: Harcourt Brace Jovanovich, 1975), p. 121.

8. During an interview in Belgrade on May 23, 1974, Djilas agreed that his definitive biography of Njegoš, published in 1966, was his best work of literature. This study demonstrated not only Djilas's political viewpoints and Romanticism, but also his deep admiration for Njegoš and his love for Montenegro. See also Milovan Djilas, *Legenda o Njegoš* [The legend of Njegoš] (Belgrade: Kultura, 1952).

9. Djilas, *Njegoš*, pp. 397–427.

10. See Günther Bartsch, *Milovan Djilas; oder die Selbstbehauptung des Menschen. Versuch einer Biographie* [Milovan Djilas; or the self-assertion of the people. An attempt at a biography] (Munich: Manz Verlag, 1971). Bartsch, an ex-Communist, was especially effective at plumbing the depths of this psychological conflict.

11. Djilas, *Land without Justice*, pp. 352–353.

12. Milovan Djilas, *Memoir of a Revolutionary*, trans. Drenka Willen (New York: Harcourt Brace Jovanovich, 1973), p. 95; and idem, *Land without Justice*, pp. 126–127, 270–277, 302–305.

13. Bartsch, *Milovan Djilas*, p. 49.

14. Ibid., p. 48. Also see Djilas, *Land without Justice*, pp. 353–357, and *Memoir of a Revolutionary*, p. 92. In a 1971 Ph.D. dissertation, John W. McDonald, Jr., unsuccessfully attempts to reconcile the aesthetic and political strains running through Djilas's intellectual make-up ("Political Themes in the Thought of Milovan Djilas," Columbia University).

15. Djilas, *Memoir of a Revolutionary*, pp. 12, 109–259.

16. Fitzroy Maclean, *The Heretic: The Life and Times of Josip Broz–Tito* (New York: Harper and Brothers, 1957), p. 375.

17. Djilas, "In the New Year," in *Parts of a Lifetime*, pp. 129–133. For other examples of his Stalinism, consult "Stalin," in ibid., pp. 303–306; and idem, *Članci, 1941–1946* [Articles, 1941–1946] (Belgrade: Kultura, 1947).

18. Interview with Djilas on May 23, 1974. For a fuller account of some of Djilas's partisan activities, see Vladimir Dedijer, *Tito* (New York: Simon and Schuster, 1953).

19. Milovan Djilas, *Conversations with Stalin*, trans. Michael B. Petrovich (New York: Harcourt, Brace and World, 1962), p. 20.

20. He was identified in the interview of May 23, 1974.

21. Djilas, *Conversations with Stalin*, pp. 50–51. This theme forms the basis for his later critiques of communism in *The New Class: An*

*Analysis of the Communist System* (New York: Frederick A. Praeger, 1957), and *The Unperfect Society: Beyond the New Class*, trans. Dorian Cooke (New York: Harcourt, Brace and World, 1969).

22. Djilas, *Conversations with Stalin*, pp. 21–22.

23. Djilas, "Perversion of the People's Power," in *Parts of a Lifetime*, pp. 162–165.

24. Vladimir Dedijer, *The Battle Stalin Lost: Memoirs of Yugoslavia, 1948–1953* (New York: Viking Press, 1970), pp. 105–108, 293–296, 322–324.

25. Djilas, "Eastern Sky," in *Parts of a Lifetime*, pp. 187–189.

26. These writings have been collected, translated, and republished in the United States in Milovan Djilas, *Anatomy of a Moral: The Political Essays of Milovan Djilas*, ed. Abraham Rothberg (New York: Frederick A. Praeger, 1959). The one omission, "Objective Forces," was recently reprinted in *Parts of a Lifetime*, pp. 206–208.

27. Djilas, "For All?" in *Anatomy of a Moral*, p. 69.

28. Djilas, "Concretely," in ibid., pp. 94–96.

29. Djilas, "League or Party," in ibid., p. 135.

30. George W. Hoffman and Fred Warner Neal, *Yugoslavia and the New Communism* (New York: Twentieth-Century Fund, 1962), pp. 189–190.

31. Djilas, "I Have Nothing More to Say," in *Parts of a Lifetime*, pp. 235–237. Djilas explained his intellectual state and recantation in a dramatic essay, written on the night of January 29, 1954 ("Nordic Dream," in ibid., pp. 243–264).

32. Djilas, *Parts of a Lifetime*, p. 289.

33. Interview with Milovan Djilas in Belgrade on May 24, 1974.

34. In addition to *Land without Justice* and *Njegoš*, *Under the Colors*, *The Stone and the Violets*, *Montenegro*, and *The Leper and Other Stories* are based largely on Montenegrin themes. See Milovan Djilas, *Under the Colors*, trans. Lovett F. Edwards (New York: Harcourt Brace Jovanovich, 1971); *Montenegro*, trans. Kenneth Johnstone (New York: Harcourt, Brace and World, 1962); and *The Leper and Other Stories*, trans. Lovett F. Edwards (New York: Harcourt, Brace and World, 1964). *Njegoš*, *Montenegro*, and *Land without Justice* "constitute a whole" about Montenegro.

35. Djilas, *The Unperfect Society*, pp. 248–250.

36. Milovan Djilas, "The Storm in Eastern Europe," *U.S. News and*

*World Report*, December 21, 1956, pp. 80–82.

37. *The New Class* is an attack on the institutionalizing abuses of communism. Preceding the all-out philosophical critique of *The Unperfect Society*, it is more objective and analytical than *Conversations with Stalin* and *The Unperfect Society*.

38. *New York Times*, November 29, 1960, p. 10.

39. Djilas, *The Unperfect Society*, p. 248.

40. Ibid., pp. 18–19.

41. Milovan Djilas, "The Communist Idea Is Dead," *Saturday Evening Post*, January 25, 1969, pp. 15–17.

42. Milovan Djilas, "Russia's Dangerous New Doctrine of Conquest," *Reader's Digest* 94 (January 1969): 43–47.

43. Djilas, *Land without Justice*, p. 324.

44. Milovan Djilas, "There'll Be Many Different Communisms in 1984," *New York Times Magazine*, March 23, 1969, p. 140.

45. Mihajlo Mihahlov, "Yugoslavia: Behind the Revelry, Retreat," *New York Times*, October 12, 1974, p. 31.

46. See John Milton, *Izgubljeni raj* [*Paradise Lost*], trans. Milovan Djilas (New York: Harcourt, Brace and World, 1969).

47. Albert Camus, *The Myth of Sisyphus*, trans. Justin O'Brien (New York: Viking Books, 1959), pp. 40–41.

48. In the Belgrade interviews with Djilas, he repeatedly stressed his realistic approach to life. See also Djilas, *The Unperfect Society*, pp. 27–35, 69–92, 251–267; and "Djilas, 'The Central Question Is Europe,'" *World* 1 (August 1973): 23.

49. Interview with Djilas on May 22, 1974, in Belgrade; Milovan Djilas, review in *Washington Post*, September 17, 1972, Book World, pp. 1–2; and idem, "On Communism and the Camps," *New York Times*, July 3, 1974, p. 31.

50. Djilas, *Land without Justice*, p. 277.

51. Djilas, *Montenegro*, p. 56.

52. Djilas, *Njegoš*, p. 416.


## SELECTED BIBLIOGRAPHY

Auty, Phyllis. *Tito*. Baltimore: Penguin Books, 1974.

Denike, Yury Petrovich. "Djilas o kommuniste" [Djilas on Communists]. *Novy Zhurnal* [New journal] 51 (1957): 217–229.

Djilas, Milovan. "Beyond Dogma." *Survey* 17 (1971): 184–188.

―――. *Lenin on Relations between Socialist States.* New York: Yugoslav Information Center, 1950.

―――. *Na novin putevima socijalizma* [On new roads to socialism]. Belgrade: Rad, 1950.

―――. "On Alienation: Thoughts on a Marxist Myth." *Encounter* 36 (May 1971): 8–15.

―――. "Reflections on Miha·lo Mihajlov's Fate." *New York Times*, November 14, 1974, p. 47.

―――. *The Threat to Yugoslavia: Discussion in the Ad Hoc Political Committee of the United Nations Organization, Sixth Session.* Belgrade, 1952.

―――. "A World Atlas for 2024." *Saturday Review World*, August 24, 1974, pp. 25–26.

Goldfield, Ethel. "Milovan Djilas: Disillusioned Communist." Ph.D. dissertation, University of Montreal, 1963.

Hammond, Thomas Taylor. "The Djilas Affair and Jugoslav Communism." *Foreign Affairs* 33 (January 1955): 298–315.

Mihajlov, Mihajlo. "Djilas versus Marx: The Theory of Alienation." *Survey* 18 (1972): 1–13.

Morgan, Dan. "Walking and Talking with Milovan Djilas." *Washington Post*, May 31, 1973, sec. A, p. 22.

*Pregled istoriia saveza komunista jugoslavije* [Summary history of the League of Yugoslav Communists]. Belgrade: IRP, 1963.

Ruberto, Robert. "A Conversation with Djilas." *Partisan Review* 38 (1971): 449–457.

Ströhm, Carl Gustav. "Encounter with Milon Djilas." In *Kontinent*, ed. Vladimir Maximov, pp. 35–38. Garden City, N.Y.: Anchor Press/Doubleday, 1976.

Sulzberger, C. L. "Foreign Affairs: Rebel's Rebel." *New York Times*, May 26, 1968, sec. 4, p. 18.

Vukmanović-Tempo, Svetozar. *Revolucija koja teče: Memoari* [The ongoing revolution: Memoirs]. Belgrade: "Komunist," 1971.

# The Fading Dream: How European Revolutionaries Have Seen the American Revolution

*R. R. Palmer*

It is an honor and a pleasure to be the invited speaker for the eleventh Walter Prescott Webb Memorial Lectures, which prompts me to recall the all too brief acquaintance that I had with Professor Webb. He was president of the American Historical Association in 1958. Somehow I met him at that time, and I well remember the presidential address that he gave, in the ornate and high-ceilinged grand ballroom of the Mayflower Hotel in Washington. His address was more enjoyable and refreshing than these staid performances usually are. It was also more autobiographical. Walter Webb professed a humorous amazement at standing on the spot that he occupied that evening.

He had had an extraordinary career. Since I had always been a library scholar myself, operating within strictly academic channels, I was fascinated by the account of a man who had come to history from the plains of West Texas and whose researches had been conducted, in part, in conversations with cowboys. His youth had been uncertain and difficult. He taught for years in the Texas public schools, then began as an instructor at the University of Texas at the age of thirty. He was forty-five when he went through the orthodox ritual of receiving a Ph.D. He had already published one of his two most famous books, *The Great Plains*, and soon produced the other, *The Texas Rangers*. These made him one of the founders of the modern serious study of the history of the American West. He was Harmsworth Professor at Oxford in 1942, president of what was then called the Mississippi Valley Historical Association in 1953, and received the American Council of Learned Societies Special Award in 1958, the year of his presidency of the American Historical Association. His death in 1963 was tragically unforeseen, but hardly premature, since he was seventy-five years old and loaded with honors.

He also wrote a book called *The Great Frontier*. I found it especially interesting, though it was too summarily dismissed in the historical journals. In it he attempted to apply to the European world as a whole, since the fifteenth century, the idea of the frontier as applied by Turner and others to the history of the United States. He showed how Europe had been transformed by its own expanding frontier, that is, the development of the ocean trade routes, the challenge to innovation and enterprise, the accumulation of wealth from the exploitation of vast new lands, the colonization of the Americas, the increased commerce with Asia, the new foods and medicines brought to Europe, the new geographical knowledge, and the revelation of great alternative civilizations which caused Europeans to perceive themselves in a different light. It was a bold and ambitious book, admittedly imperfect in execution. For example, it said nothing of the importance of African slavery in the development of the Americas, and indeed there was something shaky in the concept of the frontier itself. The overseas frontier of Europe, when made to include all Latin America, the Caribbean, Asia, and Africa, was not much like the frontier in the United States, an adjacent area into which persons of the same language or population group moved out to settle and civilize it.

Yet Walter Webb was one of the few professors of history in this country, among whom I would include my own mentor, Carl Becker, who attempted to deal with American and European history at the same time. Since I was trying to do something of the same kind when his book came out, I was impressed by the magnitude of his vision. And this brings me to my subject, which is how Europe was affected by the American Revolution. Its comparative approach to history offers a particular case of what Walter Webb was aiming at in his *Great Frontier.*

No one need be reminded that this is also the Bicentennial year of the American Revolution. The planners of these lectures, however, have decided that the subject for this year shall be revolutions and revolutionaries in Europe. What I say should fall under both headings. It may serve as a Bicentennial observance, but it is really about Europe and Europeans. More especially, it is about Europeans who have favored the possibility of revolution in their own countries, that is, the European Left. Two centuries ago those who had revolutionary ideas in Europe looked upon the new United States with enthusiasm. They saw America in an idealistic glow; it was a source of inspiration —a mirage, a vision, or a dream. Today, on the Left, the dream has faded. For some, it has turned into a nightmare. The United States is seen as a counterrevolutionary country, which indeed it is, if revolution is equated with communism. Henry Kissinger has been called the new Metternich, and probably he has seen himself in this role, since in his professorial days, twenty years ago, he wrote a book in which Metternich was the hero because he labored to stabilize the world after the French revolutionary and Napoleonic upheavals.

The change of attitude in Europe toward the American Revolution has been gradual over the years and is due both to changes in America itself and to changes in the nature of revolution. Let me begin with a remark by Karl Marx, written in the 1860s, at about the half-way point between the American Revolution and our own time. He mentioned America in the preface to the first German edition of *Das Kapital.* "As the American War of Independence of the eighteenth century," said Marx, "gave the storm signal for the European middle class, so the American Civil War of the nineteenth century has given the storm signal for the European working class." He made the remark casually and out of context, and judging from the index to his forty-volume works I do not think that he ever developed the thought at any length.

Yet a few observations can be made. The "storm signal" means the signal for revolution. There are two such signals, for a second revolution is expected to follow the first. The events of 1776 are called a war of independence, not a revolution; the American Revolution has always been hard to fit into a Marxist pattern of class struggle in a Marxist sense. Yet it activated revolutionary efforts in Europe, most especially in France in 1789. Here I think that Marx was essentially right: the American Revolution did have this effect, and both the French Revolution and accompanying disturbances of that time, in Holland, Belgium, Switzerland, Italy, Poland, Ireland, and Great Britain itself, can in the last analysis be thought of as middle-class movements. That the American Civil War gave the signal for a working-class revolution has proved to be mistaken. It is true that during our Civil War the European working class was more sympathetic to the North, and to the maintenance of an undivided United States, than were most of the European governments and ruling groups. But the American Civil War did not really herald a European working-class revolution. Nor can it be said that the Civil War prefigured a revolutionary working-class movement in America, except possibly by an exercise in dialectics, in which it is argued that the war advanced the process of industrialization and concentration of capital, from which, a priori, a revolutionary proletariat had to emerge. In fact, America and its working class proved a great disappointment to European socialist intellectuals in the generation after Marx's death. By the end of the nineteenth century the American and European revolutionary traditions had diverged.

It is this divergence that I wish to explore, but first it is necessary to observe how in the eighteenth century the American and European revolutionary movements were alike. It is here that we find the dream that was eventually to fade.

Not only were the Americans the first people to rebel against a European colonial empire; they also were seen in Europe as working out the ideas of the Enlightenment. They fought for liberty against despotism and for equality against privilege. They rejected history and the past. In setting up their new governments they seemed to be putting the principle of the social contract into practice. The sovereignty of the people was their watchword. They claimed to be able to govern themselves; they issued declarations of rights; and they drew up brief and rational constitutions, first in their several states and then in the federal constitution of 1787. They created machinery for elections, voting rights, and representative government; they held that all powers of office were delegated and temporary and believed that government officials could be removed by the will of the voters. People of all religions lived peaceably side by side. The farmer owned his land without paying manorial dues to a lord or tithes to a church. The Americans were thought to be uncorrupted by the luxurious ways of the old Europe, and there was much effusive talk about American simplicity and virtue. It is true that there were then no rich people in America at all comparable to the wealthy in Europe, but Europeans outdid themselves in praising the modesty of the American standard of living. In a word, the Americans were happily free from everything that liberal Europeans objected to—irremovable and secret government, hereditary aristocracy, and ecclesiastical power. Nor were there wide differences between rich and poor.

America thus came to symbolize the hopes of the revolution in Europe that followed within a few years after the independence of the United States.[1] Most of the French revolutionaries of 1789 were warm friends of the new republic. The story of this rage for America has often been told, and endless quotations could be assembled. Lafayette, Mirabeau, Condorcet, Brissot, Madame Roland, Du Pont de Nemours, before becoming prominent in the French Revolution, clarified their ideas or excited their feelings in discussing the American Revolution.

Proof was found in America for the right of revolution itself. "There is no authority," said the Abbé Raynal in 1781, "created yesterday or a thousand years ago, which cannot be abrogated in ten years or tomorrow."[2] There was the argument for the universality of rights. "The spectacle of a great people among whom the rights of man are respected," said Condorcet in 1788, "is useful to all other peoples despite differences of climate, customs, and constitutions. It teaches that these rights are everywhere the same."[3] Condorcet was caught on the losing side in the French Revolution five years later. There was the argument that a vast and portentous event had occurred in world history. "Not a particular or passing interest is at stake here, but the interest of all peoples now existing, and of all ages to come."[4] These words were written in 1784 by a young lawyer at Toulouse, in a prize-winning essay entitled a *Discourse on the Greatness and Importance of the Recent Revolution in North America*. The author played an important role in the trial and death of Louis XVI in 1793. Other writings were composed in verse, and I will venture on a couple of more or less poetical translations. Verse in those days could also convey arguments, and there was the argument for equality. America was,

*A land without difference of rank or of birth,*
*Where the honest and useful are the men of most worth.*[5]

This writer was an interpreter in the French foreign office, who resented the monopolizing of higher positions by the upper classes. Another versifier wrote a whole epic poem on the American Revolution, in the course of which he exclaimed, addressing the Americans,

*May the world as a whole, aroused by your laws,*
*Recover its rights in a great common cause.*[6]

Other countries than France shared in the excitement. In England, Richard Price wrote a book to argue that other peoples would soon be freed by the American example. There were warm partisans of America in the Dutch Netherlands, as John Adams found when he was American minister there in 1780; he likewise did more to foment revolution in Holland than Thomas Jefferson ever did when he was minister to France a few years later. Swiss philosopher Isaac Iselin observed in 1778 that "North America is the country where reason and humanity will develop more fully than anywhere else."[7] The Poles in their rebellion against Russia in 1794, and the Irish in their attempted revolution against England in 1798, thought they were following in American footsteps.

Similar sentiments were found as far away as Russia. Alexander Radishchev, known as the first Russian revolutionary, wrote a book in 1790 called *Voyage from Petersburg to Moscow*. In it he quoted the declarations of rights and the state constitutions of the United States. Since his main purpose was to criticize the more oppressive institutions of Russia, he was exiled to Siberia. But even in Siberia there were echoes of the American Revolution. It was discussed even at Irkutsk, two thousand miles east of Moscow. We know this from an eccentric American traveler, John Ledyard, who reached Irkutsk in 1788 against the wishes of the Empress Catherine. Her agents soon caught up with him there and escorted him back to the Polish border. Doubtless a wandering Connecticut Yankee was considered subversive in the tsarina's broad domain.

The affinity between European revolutionaries and the United States, at this time, can be seen also if we think of all those who emigrated to America and remained there. A French list would include Edmond Genêt, remembered in American history as Citizen Genêt, who stirred up a furor in 1793 when, as French minister to the United States, he interfered in American politics to gain support for the French Republic. He was an enthusiastic revolutionary until the Robespierrists came into power; he then chose to remain in America and lived in New York State for forty years, comfortably married into the high society of the Jeffersonian Democratic party. A French republican general, who commanded the small French force that invaded Ireland in 1798, could not stomach Napoleon Bonaparte, went to America, and fought at the battle of New Orleans under Andrew Jackson. Du Pont de Nemours did not remain in America, but his two grown sons did and greatly prospered. (Some may think that the American Du Ponts are of aristocratic French origin, since "de Nemours" may give that impression; but it was never really part of their name, for Pierre Samuel Du Pont was only the son of a clockmaker and fully involved in the French Revolution except during its most extreme phase.) Even refugee French priests, who might sympathize with the French Revolution at first, only later to be uprooted, could find a home in America and become American citizens. For example, there was Father Gabriel Richard, who reached Detroit in 1798. Finding himself perfectly able to work with a young American Presbyterian, he is remembered as one of the two co-founders of the University of Michigan in 1817, and he remains one of the few Roman Catholic priests ever to serve in the United States Congress.

Joseph Priestley, in trouble in England for his Unitarian and radical views, spent his last years in Pennsylvania. Thomas Cooper, driven from Manchester, ended up as president of the University of South

Carolina. Benjamin Vaughan, threatened with arrest in England, thereafter lived for forty years in Maine, where he left a substantial collection of books to Bowdoin College. Irish patriot Wolfe Tone lived for a while near Princeton, New Jersey, though he returned and met his death in the Irish uprising of 1798. Adrian Van der Kamp, involved in the Dutch revolutionary disturbances, emigrated to America and lived over forty years in upstate New York. Polish patriot Niemcewicz, after the failure of Kościuszko's rebellion, withdrew to America and married a New Jersey woman, though he too returned a dozen years later to assist Napoleon in the liberation of Poland. The stream of such revolutionists and revolutionary sympathizers continued through the failure of the European revolutions of 1848. As early as the 1820s there were hundreds of Germans in Texas, many of them noted for their unfavorable opinions of the German governments. By 1852 they numbered over ten thousand, and the *Zeitung* of San Antonio, published in German, was the second largest of the fifty-seven newspapers then existing in Texas.

Yet while there was all this fellow feeling between the European Left and America, it is also true that the divergence between the two began very early. It began at the time of the French Revolution, and it involved the distinction between a moderate or restrained revolution, such as the American was thought to be, and an extreme or more violent revolution, such as the French Revolution soon became. This distinction was correlated with another, according to whether the American Revolution was seen mainly as a fight for independence or as a struggle which also contributed to the development of democracy. Independence, or the mere separation from a larger political body, need not in principle imply any internal change. It may or may not be democratic. It may theoretically take place without commotion or extremism. There were some in America in 1776 who favored separation from England without wanting anything that might be called democratization. There have been Americans ever since who preferred this view. But, as it turned out, our revolution contributed to both independence and democracy. It proclaimed an ambivalent message. Liberty meant liberation both from foreign control and from internal restraints. Equality meant equality of Americans with the British, but also equality among Americans themselves. Later revolutionaries in Europe and elsewhere could read the American precedent either way. Or they could read it both ways together, like those of the eighteenth century that I have already quoted.

Revolutionary movements aiming simply at independence have had a wide and lasting appeal in America. In this sense, the founders of the Confederate States of America were revolutionaries in the American tradition. So were the nationalist revolutionaries of nineteenth-century Europe, the Irish, Poles, Czechs, Hungarians, Italians, and others who looked to the United States, from which they generally received sympathetic understanding. As the first people to rebel successfully against a European colonial empire, the Americans have offered precedents, or at least talking points, for all anticolonial movements. Our leaders long favored all attempts at national liberation and frowned upon European imperialism, without asking too closely what a nation really is or whether internal social revolution might not be involved also. One thinks of Woodrow Wilson with his fourteen points and his satisfaction at the break-up of the Austro-Hungarian monarchy; or optimistic expectations of what would follow the collapse of the European colonial empires, from Argentina through Africa to India and southeast Asia; or John Kennedy's promise to go anywhere and do anything to uphold liberty throughout the world.

It is a confusing fact that anyone demanding national liberation can appeal to the American Declaration of Independence. The North Vietnamese Communists have done so; so have the whites of Rhodesia, who indeed, in 1965, used some of the language of the American Declaration of Independence, with the discreet omission of all reference to equality.[8] The precedent has become embarrassing in a world where militant Ukrainians, Palestinians, French Canadians, American blacks, and American Indians see themselves as oppressed nations, and all forms of unacceptable government are denounced as colonialist or imperialist. The United Nations is sinking from an overload of liberated nations, or microstates that are not nations at all.

But mainly the divergence of the European Left, or in fact the Left throughout the world, from the original ideas of the American Revolution has come about through changes in the nature of revolution itself and in what is meant by democracy. In the *International Encyclopedia of the Social Sciences* there is a very interesting article on "revolution." It is by Walter Laqueur of the University of London. He discusses the causes, process, phases, personnel, doctrines, and consequences of revolution, and he cites an abundance of examples in a wide comparative survey. He says nothing about the American Revolution. He sees revolution as something brought about by small determined groups, an elite or vanguard, who make long and often secret preparations, take an opportune moment for the seizure of power, and then use force to impose their view of a reconstructed society. He notes that the modern doctrine of revolution derives mainly from Marxist-Leninist sources. In this light the American Revolution was a nonevent, or only a war of independence, as Marx said in 1867. Neither social scientists nor revolutionaries in our time need pay much attention to it. At most, it is used as a precedent to legitimize the act of rebellion or seen as a distant derivative from the bourgeois revolution in England.

But the real difference lies in the difference of meaning attached to "democracy." Today it is East Germany that is the German Democratic Republic. West Germany is only "federal." Personally I think that West Germany is the more democratic, but I do not suppose that the East German government is merely hypocritical, and I concede them the right to call their regime democratic, as long as we understand what we are talking about. In one sense, a system is democratic if it allows for constitutional and representative government, free elections in a competition between political parties, unintimidated voting, fair judicial procedure, free discussion in the press and other media, recognized rights for various interest groups and social classes, and a dispersion of economic power through ownership of capital by individuals and institutions outside the machinery of the state.

In the other sense, these features are subordinated or rejected. Public authorities, whose personnel is not subject to change by popular voting, act in the name of the people, which is understood to be composed of workers, since class differences have disappeared, by definition, with the disappearance of private ownership of the means of production. There is no political life in the sense of contested elections; dissent beyond a certain point is illegitimate because contrary to the public interest; the public authorities define this interest and assume total control of the intellectual, cultural, and economic life of the country. Regimes of the latter type call themselves socialist, to the embarrassment of socialists and social democrats in Western Europe and elsewhere. Most of them have resulted from revolution in Walter Laqueur's sense of the word or from revolution combined with intervention by the Soviet Union. In these countries it is not felt that the American Revolution contributed much to democracy; they look back rather to the Russian Revolution of 1917 or ultimately to the French Revolution in its radical phase of 1793. Democratic regimes of the more liberal type may think well of the American Revolution when reminded of it, but they feel more historic connection with the French Revolution of 1789.

As long as the European Left was mainly concerned with constitutional reform, representative government, and individual liberty and opposed to monarchy, aristocracy, feudalism, and a powerful church, a sense of American inspiration might be felt. This was true of most of the nineteenth-century national movements in Europe. It was true of liberals and democrats in England and France. It was true in Russia, where the Decembrists, the unsuccessful revolutionary group of 1825, proposed a constitution resembling the American federal constitution. Similar voices might have been heard in the Russian Constituent Assembly of 1918 if it had not been suppressed by Lenin.

It was the appearance of socialism, and especially of revolutionary socialism, in the middle of the last century that did most to estrange the European Left from America. Socialism is a broad term, and the Left embraces many shades of opinion, so that nothing that might be said would apply in all cases. Something can be learned, however, from the example of Karl Kautsky. As a youth in the 1870s he planned a doctoral dissertation at the University of Vienna, and after finding some old copies of the writings of Jefferson and Washington in a Vienna bookstore he decided to write about Jefferson, who interested him both as a participant in the American Revolution and as one who had been present in Paris during the French Revolution of 1789. Kautsky soon gave up the project, partly because no other books were available in Vienna on the subject, but also, as he tells in his memoirs, because he made a new acquaintance, a banker's son, who enabled him to pursue an active revolutionary career. Forty years later, still a convinced Marxist, Kautsky repudiated the Bolshevik Revolution for its violence and brutality. He wrote a book to argue that a Marxist revolution was possible without such deplorable methods. It was all about the French Revolution and the Paris commune. The American Revolution was never mentioned.[9]

But the divergence began, as already noted, with the French Revolution itself. The program of 1789, constitutionalist and liberal in its aims, was followed by the more radical phase of 1793 with its dictatorship and its terror. The radical phase was a means of protecting the earlier phase against foreign intervention and internal subversion, but it aroused excited patriots and extreme revolutionaries throughout the country. For a few months the government condoned violent popular insurrection; it created a citizen army, set up price controls and requisitions to manage the economic system, and adopted other measures to attach the poorer classes to the revolution. It proclaimed universal manhood suffrage without practicing it, and it created the idea of a revolutionary dictatorship as a means of introducing a future democratic society. It repressed all who opposed it and put quite a few to death, including a good many who had been active revolutionaries up to that point. It sent Louis XVI to the guillotine, it strove to turn Frenchmen into good republicans, and it defeated the foreign invaders. This regime lasted less than two years. But it is to this regime that the revolutionary Left in Europe has looked back with the greatest satisfaction. The first French Revolution of 1789 seemed pale beside it, and the American Revolution seemed to be no revolution at all.

It is at this time, too, in the France of the 1790s, that we find the emergence of the two senses of the word *democratic*. Robespierre often used the word *democracy* to explain what he had in mind, and I do not question his honesty of intention, or even the temporary need for some of the things that he did; but it is impossible to believe that the regime of 1794 would ever have produced a working democracy. Two years later Babeuf, in his *Conspiracy of Equals*, used the word *democracy* even more frequently than Robespierre did. Only it was to be a real democracy this time. He aimed at the abolition of private property and at a real equality of income and material goods in place of the allegedly false equality hitherto proclaimed by the French Revolution. Babeuf and his followers could never have been elected to anything even by a universal suffrage, since too many Frenchmen had an interest in keeping or enlarging their own possessions. He therefore envisaged a revolutionary dictatorship to be exercised by himself and his fellows. He is accepted on the Left as a precursor to communism and is enshrined in the ideology of the modern democratic people's republics.

French historians today, most of whom if they specialize in the French Revolution incline to the Left in their politics, call the regime of 1793–94 the democratic phase of the revolution. The arrangements of 1789, or of the Directory after 1795, are described as bourgeois. In matters of free elections, a free press, a tolerance of dissent, or acceptance of diversity in human society, the regime of 1793–94 was of course the least democratic phase of the Revolution. It was democratic only in its overwhelming emphasis on the need of equality, a true value indeed, but one to which all other values were sacrificed—those of religion, personal liberty, personal security, social peace, nonconformist opinions, individual distinction, special accomplishment, even the arts and sciences and the amenities of a traditional culture. In the French Revolution this "democratic" phase lasted only two years. It has proved more permanent in our modern people's democracies.

From such a point of view the American Revolution was bound to seem very moderate. In fact it had not been very moderate, for it had involved a civil struggle among Americans themselves as well as a war against Britain and, hence, a good deal of intimidation, repression, emigration, and confiscation of property. Yet it undoubtedly was dwarfed by the French Revolution. The French had far more grievances to correct, a more complex society to deal with, more entrenched interests to overcome, and a war against the combined powers of Europe on which the outcome of their revolution depended. Comparatively speaking the American Revolution was "moderate."

As a concluding irony it may be observed that the moderation of the American Revolution, both real and exaggerated, became a favorite idea in conservative as well as radical circles. For radicals it was too moderate to be of much continuing interest. For conservatives, to praise its moderation offered a convenient way to discredit the French Revolution. As early as 1789 the members of the French National Assembly began to differ on the use of American precedents. Those who wanted a two-house legislature, and who pointed to the American examples, were condemned as backsliders or moderates, because in

France an upper house might favor the nobles. With good reason, those who persisted in the French Revolution found less and less relevance in the American example. On the other hand, conservatives, or distressed liberals who could not accept the French regime of 1793, or revolutionaries like Brissot and Madame Roland who found themselves outflanked on the Left, continued to find a relevancy in the American Revolution, compared to which the French Jacobins could be portrayed as raging fanatics.

Friedrich Gentz wrote a book comparing the two revolutions to this effect in 1800, and Hannah Arendt said much the same in her book *On Revolution* in 1963. Actually the comparison for this purpose is irrelevant. The circumstances in France and America were too different. If the French were to make significant change in their Old Regime they could not do it by American methods. It is usually forgotten, too, that in the American Revolution the foreign intervention was on the side of the revolutionaries, in the French Revolution massively against them. The vaunted moderation of the American Revolution can be explained in part by French aid and the arrival of the French army. On the other hand, intervention against a revolution has an inflammatory effect. It is like calling the police onto a college campus; it radicalizes the moderates, at least temporarily; and this is what happened in France in 1792.

The dream of a momentous world renewal, evoked by the American Revolution, so vivid in Europe in the 1780s thus gradually faded away. True revolutionaries found more pertinent examples. Others admired the United States for reasons other than its revolutionary past. In the 1830s Alexis de Tocqueville wrote his two famous volumes, *Democracy in America*. He thought that America was the land of equality, he saw the United States as an exemplary democracy, and he hoped to draw from it useful lessons for France and Europe. But he assigned little importance to the American Revolution, which is scarcely mentioned in his thousand pages. He said, in fact, that in contrast to France the Americans had always been equal, since the earliest days of settlement on the new continent. In his words, "they were born equal and needed no revolution to become so." It was not quite true, and Tocqueville was well aware of the limits of this sweeping proposition, especially in his account of the less than equal status of American blacks and American Indians. He also understated the depth of the conflict during the revolution among the American whites. Yet there was a comparative truth in his great generalization, which he made only to bring out the contrast with France.

A successful revolution produces a new society, which in turn grows old. The more successful the revolution, the less there is likely to be talk of further revolution after the event. Today the real revolutionaries who call on the name of Lenin do not live in the Soviet Union. In the eighteenth century the English who most benefited from the discords of the preceding century were politically very conservative. So it is in a way with the American Revolution. We quite properly observe its Bicentennial, with more pious respect than actual fervor. Politicians and journalists may talk of carrying the American Revolution to the rest of the world, though less audibly than a few years ago; but it is not clear what this revolution consists of or whether the world wants it. A few avowed revolutionaries may say that we need a new American Revolution and even applaud the violence that occurred in the 1770s, but real revolutions are not made by fringe groups or by historical references. The United States today has overwhelming problems, but it does not expect to solve them by revolution.

In Europe, if the American Revolution has receded, not only on the Left but also elsewhere, the United States has nevertheless exerted an influence due indirectly and in the long run to what our eighteenth-century predecessors accomplished. It has been seen as the land of the common people and has attracted great streams of immigration. It long stood as the country of busy technical civilization, the home of the popular motor car, the quick lunch, and the high-rise building, before Europe had such things for itself. It has been admired for its equality, which remains a powerful force in this country; for its efficiency, which let us hope can be restored; and for its power, which we must hope will be wisely used. These have all flowed from the success of the American Revolution. So there is still something for Americans to celebrate, and for Europeans to think about.

NOTES

1. In general, for the following paragraphs, see my *Age of the Democratic Revolution: A Political History of Europe and America* (Prince-

ton: Princeton University Press, 1959), chap. 9, "Europe and the American Revolution," which contains references and documentation. See also the various papers in the Library of Congress Bicentennial Symposium for 1975, *The Impact of the American Revolution Abroad* (Washington, D.C., 1976). References are given in the following pages only for direct quotations.

2. G. T. Raynal, *La Révolution de l'Amérique* (Paris, 1781), p. 20.

3. A. N. Condorcet, *Oeuvres complètes*, 12 vols. (Paris, 1847–49), 8:29.

4. J. B. Mailhe,*Discours sur la grandeur et l'importance de la Révolution qui vient de s'opérer dans l'Amérique Septentrionale* (Toulouse, 1784), p. 4.

5. L. G. Bourdon, *Voyage d'Amérique: Dialogue en vers entre l'auteur et l'abbe* (Paris, 1786), p. 23.

6. Chavanne de la Giraudière, *L'Amérique Delivrée: Esquisse d'un poëme sur l'indépendance de l'Amérique* (Amsterdam, 1783), p. 718.

7. G. Steiner, ed., *Korrespondenz des Peter Ochs*, 3 vols. (Basel: H. Opperman, 1927–1937), 1:104.

8. The reader may be interested in this textual curiosity: "Whereas in the course of human affairs history has shown that it may become necessary for a people to resolve [*sic*] the political affiliations that have connected them with another people, and to assume amongst other nations the separate and equal status to which they are entitled . . ." (Kenneth Young, *Rhodesia and Independence* [London: Eyre & Spottiswoode, 1967], p. 286).

9. See K. Kautsky's *Erinnerungen und Erörterungen* (The Hague: Mouton, 1960), pp. 396–400, and his *Terrorism and Communism: A Contribution to the Natural History of Revolution*, trans. W. H. Kerridge (London: Allen and Unwin, 1920).

# National Sovereignty at the Bar: Revolution by Law?

*George Barr Carson, Jr.*

On February 20, 1975, the Court of Justice of the European Communities reported two decisions, one in favor of Jeanne Airola and the other against Chantal Van den Broeck.[1] Each had sued the Commission of the European Communities, by which she was employed, claiming discrimination. But the alleged discrimination was not over a simple matter of equal pay for equal work; Airola and Van den Broeck objected to the fact that, as females, each had incurred upon marriage an arbitrary legal change in nationality owing to the law of her husband's paricular state, whereas no male, upon marriage, incurred any change in nationality under the law in any member state of the European Communities.

The importance of principle involved in the two suits should not be diminished, but there was also a matter of money. The staff regulations for employees of the institutions of the European Communities provided for a supplementary pay allowance in certain circumstances when a national of one member state took a post in a European Communities agency located on the territory of a different member state. What might be called the "hardship" supplement applied equally, for example, to a German employed in Paris or an Englishman in Dublin because they were required to live outside their countries of nationality. Airola, a Belgian subject, had been working for the commission at the Joint Research Center at Ispra in Italy, receiving the stipulated differential for residence in a state other than that of her nationality, when she married an Italian citizen, also employed by the commission at Ispra. She continued in her job, but the commission suspended her foreign-resident supplement; under Italian law Airola automatically acquired her husband's nationality and could not renounce it.[2] Under Belgian law, however, Airola could, upon marrying a non-Belgian subject, elect to retain her Belgian nationality, a choice she had duly made and properly recorded. She wanted her pay maintained at her premarriage level, as a Belgian working for the commission in Italy.

The Court of Justice of the European Communities does not alter the laws of the member states. But its decision in *Airola* v. *Commission* implied that changes were needed. In finding for Airola the court reported: "The concept of 'nationals' contained in Article 4(a) of Annex VII of the Staff Regulations of officials must be interpreted in such a way as to avoid any unwarranted difference of treatment as between male and female officials who are, in fact, placed in comparable situations. It is, therefore, necessary to exclude nationality imposed by law on a female official upon her marriage with a national of another State and which she was unable to renounce."[3]

Although the circumstances seemed identical, in Van den Broeck's case the court dismissed her suit. She failed because under a Franco-Belgian agreement she had the opportunity to renounce the Belgian nationality that would automatically be conferred upon her by marriage and retain her French citizenship, provided she did so within a six-month period. Since she had not done so, the court judged she had accepted the change from French to Belgian nationality effected by her marriage, and the commission correctly applied the staff regulations when it suspended her foreign-resident supplement.

Clearly the court could not have it both ways—upholding Van den Broeck's claim, although she had not taken the legal option open to her, as well as that of Airola, who had. But the more subtle point here is that the court was affirming once again a principle that it had steadfastly maintained in its decisions for more than two decades and that had been accepted in the courts of the member states: that nationality, one of the pillars of the European revolutionary tradition since 1789, may not be used to limit equality, another pillar of the European revolutionary tradition, in the European Communities.

The outstanding significance for the European revolutionary tradition in the formation of the European Communities was in its breach of the prevailing sanctity of nationalism in international organizations. The "fraternity" of the original French revolutionary trilogy—liberty, equality, fraternity—had very quickly been limited to fraternity only within the borders of national states. As a consequence of the rise of nationalism and of the nation-state as the primary unit in international society, the great experiments in international organization in the first half of the twentieth century had preserved virtually intact the principle of national sovereignty. The first of the European communities, the European Coal and Steel Community (ECSC), established by the Treaty of Paris in 1951, broke the precedent; it provided for an important, albeit limited, transfer by the member states of the exercise of some of their sovereignty to the institutions of the new community. Thus, more than 150 years elapsed after the great upheaval at the close of the eighteenth century before the European Communities began to break down the barriers which a distorted version of fraternity had thrown up against the universal implementation of liberty and equality in the European revolutionary tradition.

The pattern for the structure of the European Communities was set by the institutions of the original European Coal and Steel Community. These new institutions were an administrative board, called the High Authority, whose members, once selected, were independent of the governments in their respective countries; a Council of Ministers, which consisted usually of the foreign ministers of the member states (Belgium, the Federal Republic of Germany, France, Italy, Luxembourg, and the Netherlands) and approved regulations to implement the Treaty of Paris; an Assembly, whose members were selected by the legislatures of the member states in proportion to size, organized according to *political parties* and not according to national contingents; an Economic and Social Committee, whose members represented labor and employer groups; and a Court of Justice, whose members were also, while in office, independent of the governments of their own states. The significance of the new Court of Justice was that its jurisdiction extended not simply to governments, but also to enterprises and individuals in all the member states, in any matter arising out of the treaties establishing the communities.

In 1957 the Treaty of Rome created two more communities, with the same member states as the ECSC: the European Economic Community (EEC), universally known as the Common Market because its primary purpose was to facilitate an economic and customs union, and the European Atomic Energy Community (Euratom). The administrative board for these communities was called a commission instead of a high authority, but the institutions were otherwise identical with those of the ECSC. The existing Court of Justice served all three communities. In 1965 the Treaty of Brussels fused the institutions of the three communities, henceforth known as the European Communities. The enlargement of the communities in 1972 added the United Kingdom, Eire, and Denmark to the six original member states. The Treaty of Rome had provided for a transitional period before all sections came into full effect, with 1970 as the last deadline. The new member states were allowed a short transitional period after the enlargement of the communities in 1972.

Ultimate political union in some form was implied in the formation of the European Communities, and a summit conference of heads of government expressly affirmed the goal in October 1972 at Paris. The 1951 Treaty of Paris had used language that was fairly explicit in conceding supranational authority to the ECSC. The language of the Treaty of Rome was more modified, but the conception of a new community to which the member states in fact transferred the exercise of their sovereignty in limited degree was retained.

The revolutionary tradition at issue stems from the eighteenth-century movements that gave the framework to modern European society. They include the political revolution that destroyed the Old Regime of feudal privilege and absolute monarchy; the industrial revolution that displaced the agrarian society of several milleniums' standing; and the social revolution that aborted in the eighteenth century, smoldered on a long fuse in the nineteenth century, and erupted again in the twentieth century.

This European revolutionary tradition was inseparable from violence and change. Since 1789 the two have been considered inextricably linked, and today's self-styled revolutionists generally regard violence as the *sine qua non* for revolutionary change. This point of view should be challenged, because in important respects it distorts two centuries of European revolutionary development. That kind of revolution which results in the violent change of government leaders is evident enough in the history of Europe but is not peculiar to Europe. Violent change of rulers is commonplace in world history, even violent restructuring of government, although in such cases the change may be more apparent than real since it often takes place in short time spans and simply masks a new application of authoritarian leadership. On the other hand, if a radical change is viewed as being none the less a revolution for taking place over an extended period of time, then the definition of the European revolutionary tradition acquires distinctive traits not readily discernible in other regions. The Industrial Revolution, in the classic account, extended from 1760 to 1830. Subsequent historians have extended the limits earlier and later; today one can argue that it is still continuing or that it is not a revolution at all. In any case, the elements of the European tradition which stand out in that example of revolution are the factor of time and the factor of dynamic rather than abrupt change. The development of the European Communities is in the same category.

The eighteenth-century writers on social and political reform who prepared the program for the great revolutionary upheaval of 1789 emphasized the long-term and continuing character of the change they advocated. Not the details but the spirit of their revolutionary contribution is summed up in the phrase "the idea of progress." The miseries of the human race were largely attributable to its institutions, which created inequality of status, wealth, and education; by changing its institutions society's inequities could be remedied and perhaps ultimately even human nature itself transformed. And, in addition to the idea of progressive perfectibility, the reformers focused attention on property as the natural right upon which individual liberty and security depended. The focus on property rights has persisted and permeates the institutions of the European Communities.

The reform writers who contributed the intellectual background for the revolutionary movement took sweeping views of human history and human society. The revolutionaries were much more pragmatic in their approach to change. Concerned fundamentally with altering existing society to bring it more in line with what a society *ought to be*, they were willing to use violence to accomplish that end. Undeniably, the success of violence, at numerous stages in the French Revolution of 1789 and in the many lesser nineteenth-century revolutions in Europe, produced a strong tradition that violence was effective in promoting desirable change. Violence as a means was part of the legacy of the French Revolution in Europe, and the Russian Revolution in the twentieth century gave it new impetus. This part of the legacy is the most colorful, attracts the most attention, and arouses the most controversy. It has given rise in the recent literature of sociology and political science to important and interesting theoretical speculation on violence and alienation, coercion and aims, and the failure of social change.[4]

Emphasis on the legacy of violence often distracts us from the actual underlying changes. Chief among these changes is the way in which the interpretation of property and property rights is altered—revolutionized—through novel instrumentalities, such as the European Communities, to make the legal framework of society meet the social demands of security when the old interpretation no longer accomplishes that objective for the mass of the population.

"Liberty, equality, fraternity" is a popular slogan to describe the goals of the French Revolution. What these words meant in eighteenth-century terms becomes much clearer in the language of the great revolutionary documents, especially the Declaration of the Rights of Man and the Citizen, which Georges Lefebvre described as the death certificate of the Old Regime.[5] What the Old Regime died of was failure to fulfill its purpose in society: "The aim of all political association is to preserve the natural and imprescriptible rights of man; these rights are liberty, property, security, and resistance to oppression." And the greatest of these rights was property, since property can be defined as a system of social security.

To understand the right to property as an instrument of social security requires a social context. Eighteenth-century Europe was still a predominantly agrarian society with land as the chief basis of wealth. The fine-spun theory of the natural rights school, in so far as it fitted any actual rather than imaginary society, was a theory for an agrarian society. To have some property (i.e., land) meant that one could have liberty; one could support life by one's own labor on the land and be free of dependence upon anyone else. Equality meant no special privileges, with the law known to all and equally applied. Since it was labor which gave value to anything, the protection of property actually meant the protection of the fruits of labor and of the right to life and freedom from the violence of others in carrying on one's labor. But at its height in the eighteenth century the theory was not, nor was it intended to be, a description of reality. It was a rational exercise to justify the nature of civil government or to foment change in it. The nature of the relationship between individuals and the state was the fundamental question which the theory of the social contract and the theory of natural rights were designed to illuminate. And the right of property provided the linchpin of the whole structure, the basis for political organization.

In eighteenth-century Europe the prevailing system of property rights satisfactorily met the social security requirement for only a few, owing to the survival of feudal forms of proprietorship and special privileges. The change needed in property rights was the introduction of equality. In this regard the Civil Code, published under Napoleon, was the most significant and the most permanent of the revolutionary achievements, despite the flamboyant violence of the 1790s over constitutional forms. The vestiges of feudal property rights and inequality of status were abolished. That is, they were abolished for the male population; the inequality of females, legally enshrined in the Civil Code, remained for twentieth-century reformers to work on and for the Court of Justice of the European Communities to ameliorate. But the concept of equality before the law—liberty in the sense of everyone equally free to do what the law allowed, and the justification given by the theory of natural rights for a universal extension of this liberty and equality—was a lasting gain for the modern world.

The many distortions imposed on the key concept of equality, partly from political, partly from economic, and partly from social considerations, have provided ample grist for revolutionary millers. Two forces in particular, industrialism and nationalism, were the most fruitful sources of new conflict and new inequality. The first changed the basis of wealth in society, and both limited liberty and equality. The new forms of wealth could be, and were, incorporated into the equal legal protection of property rights. But in contrast to the agrarian society in which the proprietor of land could, ideally, be independent of others, not even in theory could the proprietor of machines, or the machine worker, be self-sufficient. The hard-won sovereignty of the individual, free from arbitrary interference of the Old Regime state and church, equal in rights with any other individual, became illusory in the industrial world where individuals depended upon others for their very existence. Property rights needed redefining if they were to constitute a social security system. The socialist contributions to solving the problem of social justice in an industrial, rather than an agrarian, world were to recognize the interdependence of individuals, to advocate the fusion of private and public law in property relationships, and to attack the fragmentation of society and of social justice entailed in the sovereign national state.

The nation-state, another product of the revolutionary tradition, was an extension of the sovereignty of the individual to the sovereignty of nationalities. Sovereignty of the individual and sovereignty of the nationality both had constructive inspiration in the ideal of liberty, understood as freedom for individuals, or nationalities, to develop to their fullest capacity when liberated from the oppression or constraint of others. Unfortunately, although society has always recognized the necessity of imposing regulation on the individual in the interest of the whole, it has been very slow to accept the corresponding necessity to restrict the untrammeled independence of nationalities in the same interest. Nationalism and the sovereign nation-state were the fruits of revolutionary violence in an even greater degree than the liberty and equality of the individual. National unification movements, and political independence movements by national minorities, all succeeded by resort to violence, a somber inheritance. The cause of political unification by means of violence on a scale greater than that of national units, however, was notably unsuccessful in Europe. From the Napoleonic hegemony of 1810 to the Nazi hegemony of 1943, forcible political unification has been short-lived.

Again, this has its constructive side from the standpoint of freedom and equality; nationalism has been a bulwark against either the authoritarian or the liberal-constitutional pattern of imperial aggrandizement.

If political unification has been the weakest element in the revolutionary trilogy of liberty, equality, and fraternity, always foundering on the rocks of submerged national sovereignty despite reliance on violence, economic and social unification have fared much better. Both industrialism and capitalism were transnational in nature and based on property rights. Unlike mercantilism, laissez-faire economics was predicated not on war but on the expansion of trade. The Civil Code, with its antifeudal conception of property rights, was adopted in much of Europe despite national boundaries, providing some common ground for the later European Communities.

Yet the Civil Code and its principles of liberty and equality did not secure the social justice that the great eighteenth-century revolutionaries had expected. They could not have anticipated that the whole basis of their understanding of the sources of wealth and the relationship to them of individuals would change radically in the next century with the Industrial Revolution. But they did contribute to the revolutionary tradition a key to adaptation of individual rights to the circumstances of a changed society in their reliance on law as an instrument of social justice, especially law as a regulator of property rights in the interest of equality.

Most legal definitions of property, from the Roman *dominium* to the sophisticated modern "bundle of rights," have been concerned with rights against others with respect to anything that has a present or potential material value. Since, economically, the forms of wealth have undergone a profound change over the past two centuries, definition of rights rather than of the nature of the wealth became imperative to social security. Perhaps Jeremy Bentham went too far when he held that "till law existed, property could scarcely be said to exist. Property and law were born together and die together . . . take away law and property is at an end."[6] Eighteenth-century disciples of John Locke on natural rights did not deny that property existed in a state of nature; they argued that the establishment of law mitigated the insecurity of proprietorship. The purpose of organized society was to validate and protect claims by particular individuals to specific property. Speculation on the intricate nature of the right of property was, to most eighteenth-century revolutionaries, far less important than correcting abuses which denied equality in the right itself.

Abuses stemmed in part from the tendency in European development toward rigid separation of public and private law that had been fused in feudal society. The object of feudalism was security; landholding was organized to sustain a military caste and those dependent upon it for protection. Wealth, in the feudal notion, was measured in men, whether of war or of work. Rights and obligations were balanced; both were simultaneously public and private. The gradual transfer of the public obligations of landholders to centralized territorial monarchies left most of the rights to sources of wealth in private hands. When the lord of land came to regard it as personal wealth, he also "claimed absolute ownership and the right to do what he liked with his own."[7] The culmination of this separation of private and public right with respect to property appeared in the French Civil Code of 1804, which emphasized the absolute power of the owner implied in the Roman law concept of *dominium*.

*Dominium* describes ownership as an authority one either has or lacks, without conditions. The emphasis upon it in the late eighteenth and early nineteenth centuries coincided with the development of industrialization, the economic principles of laissez faire, the emphasis on liberty generally in the political growth of nineteenth-century liberalism and nationalism, and the emergence of the nation-state. In Hegelian terms the community of mankind was evolving gradually from status to contract and from group holding to individual property; there had been a concomitant growth in the liberty of the individual in the process. Equating growth in individual property holding with greater liberty surely emphasized "a valuable truth—he who is wholly dependent on property controlled by others in their own interest can hardly live the life of the free."[8] But where the Civil Code inheritance principles worked toward equalization of property holding in land, as they did in France, equality and liberty were both emasculated by the Industrial Revolution with its fostering of a new form of property whose ownership was still concentrated in a minority.

Few owners in civilized states today could meet the test of absolute power over property if only because of the impingement of statutory regulation on zoning, nuisance, and other amenity interests. And at least as far back as the introduction of poor rates by Tudor governments, some responsibility for social welfare has fallen on private property in some places. In modern times community control of property goes very much further: "Today we see the effective working of the institution of property, not in a mere analysis of concepts borrowed from Roman law, but in a realistic study of what legislatures and courts are actually doing. . . . What is apparent is that absolute rights are ceasing to exist, if they ever did exist, and are being replaced by qualified rights the exercise of which is limited by the philosophy and needs of the community in question."[9] It was always thus. But therein lies the danger; unless some absolute rights are recognized in theory, there is a loss of liberty, since without them the individual has no standing against the community and even popularly elected representative legislatures—as the French Revolutionary Convention demonstrated—can be just as tyrannical as Old Regime monarchs. On this point the eloquent defense of individual liberty against the tyranny of the majority made by John Stuart Mill in his essay *On Liberty* should rank him with other notable standard-bearers of the European revolutionary tradition, although he is not usually numbered among them in survey textbooks of modern civilization.

Modern governments have tended to move in some respects toward the once feudal fusion of private and public law. In the United Kingdom, for instance, rent acts, landlord and tenant acts, leasehold reform acts, and others reintroduce into land law "a conception of ownership which includes legal duties as well as legal rights."[10] The protection of a tenant against eviction, even in some instances despite inability to pay the rent, goes very far in the direction of establishing social rights analogous to civil rights; that is, they are valid as of right against the organized community unless it can show extraordinary cause for transgressing them.

The traditional property right in land is perhaps most at risk in contemporary social legislation: "The increasing tendency in modern times is not to attempt to justify the institution of private property by an *a priori* theory [for example, natural rights], but to build doctrines on an analysis of the functioning and social effects of the institution. This approach is sometimes called the functional theory, and it lays down that property which is the result of effort or involves the giving of service is ethically justifiable, but property which is an undeserved claim on the wealth produced by others is not."[11] This philosophy seems to ignore that the individual in an industrial society cannot survive otherwise than by claims on others; unless these claims are safeguarded in some way analogous to the natural rights guarantee of property right, the individual is still unequal and unfree in comparison with those who have property, even property ethically justifiable under the terms of the theory.

Some authorities suggest that, since "the term 'property' is frequently used in a broad sense to include assets which the technique of the law would regard as mere rights *in personam* . . . it would save confusion if the term 'patrimony' were used to cover the whole of a person's assets instead of thus extending the term 'property.' Patrimony would include: (a) *dominium*; (b) proprietary interests less than ownership; (c) claims upon others, e.g. obligations."[12] The concept of the *patrimoine* is indeed generally applied in French law; but although this might perhaps save technical confusion, it might also break the link with natural rights and the right to property as the chief of them.[13] From the standpoint of individual liberty, treating aspects of social security as forms of property right would therefore be preferable.

This in effect is what the courts in advanced industrial states have been doing since they began to interpret trade union–negotiated labor contracts as conferring on an individual worker a property right to his or her job. The Court of Justice of the European Communities from its beginning in 1951 extended a similar interpretation to all economic benefits for individuals within the limits of its jurisdiction. "The enforcement of property rights is a critical aspect of their existence. . . . The 'social' aspect of enforcement means that all rights have a public element."[14] If the exercise and enforcement of rights are crucial to their survival, the Court of Justice's handling of social security issues gives the European Communities a key role. Actually, national courts have the enforcement, but the Court of Justice is telling national courts how they must use it in social security claims to promote equality among all the inhabitants of the European Communities independent of nationality.

The revolutionaries since the eighteenth century have not really wanted to abolish property but to change the character or the locus of its ownership. The underlying philosophy behind the institution of property is obscured when revolutionary sloganeers describe property in real terms and proprietors as particular persons engaged in rivalry over its possession. And what the later Marxist aspect of the revolutionary movement sought to abolish was *capitalist* property (the form which had succeeded *feudal* property, abolished in the French Revolution and its aftermath), in favor of *socialist* property. But the reason was always the same—the standing that property gives its owner: "A man with much property has great bargaining strength and a great sense of security, independence, and freedom; and he enjoys these things not only *vis-à-vis* his propertyless fellow citizens but also *vis-à-vis* the public authorities. He can snap his fingers at those on whom he must rely for an income; for he can always live for a time on his capital. The propertyless man must continuously and without interruption acquire his income by working for an employer or by qualifying to receive it from a public authority."[15]

To make the concept of property as liberty truly socially useful the definition should be extended so that working for an employer or receiving support from a public authority is interpreted as a "property right" claim just as is the ownership of capital. *Then*, if property is protected against arbitrary and whimsical confiscation, the statement about "sense of security, independence, and freedom" is true for all who have any kind of property: for those whose "property" consists of claims to a job or to social security services in an industrial society no less than for those whose "property" is in the traditional means or instruments of production.

The new form of property right differs in one essential way from the more traditional form; in essence it is personal, effective only if exercised by the individual. It is a right that cannot, and should not, be alienated or hypothecated. Otherwise it would defeat its individual social security purpose and become simply another means of enabling the accumulation of property by a few without necessary benefit to others any more than in any traditional system of property ownership.

In the European Communities a principal source of inequality in programs of social security has been the difference between the varying benefits provided by the separate national schemes of the several member states. The nation-state, not the European Communities, pioneered the guarantee of legal protection to social security as a property right. But from the first discussion of the plans for a coal and steel community, one of the clearly stated basic objectives was to accelerate a rise in the standard of living and to promote more equitable distribution of income and use of the national product.[16] The administration of the national social security systems remained with the member states and differences in social security systems still exist, but the gap is closing gradually through the program of "harmonization" mandated in Article 117 of the Treaty of Rome.

The extent of the gap between social services in the member states in 1958 was not apparent in the overall comparative figures but in specific types of benefit. All the participating countries spent proportions of GNP in amounts ranging from 10.6 percent to 14.1 percent, a discrepancy which by itself was not a serious hindrance to harmonization. The range between the country paying out the lowest and the country paying out the highest proportion of its GNP in social services was still 3.5 percent fifteen years later, but in that interval the proportion of GNP devoted to such expenditures went up by more than half: from an average 12 percent in 1958 to 15 percent in 1962 and 19 percent in 1970. The overall disparity thus became smaller, since the difference of 3.5 percent is within a higher proportion of GNP, which has itself also risen but at a less rapid pace than social expenditures. Coverage against sickness and other social security measures have been extended to a greater proportion of the population during the same period.

Where the goal of closer alignment in social security systems had most effect was in the distribution of the amounts extended between different categories of aid: "For health insurance, the gap between the highest and lowest proportion of the total [spent on social services] was [1958] 13–26 and is now [1970] 22–31; for old-age benefits, the corresponding figures are 32–47 and 37–45; and even for family allowances, largely owing to the considerable reduction in the proportion in France and Italy, the change is from 7–30 to 8–21."[17] Although the spectacular decrease in the differences between countries did not result from any Community directive, a permanent documentation system facilitates information exchange between national governments, industry, and labor organizations. The Community's mere existence has contributed to a more competitive situation in social security schemes. But the distribution of resources between different social categories encounters significantly differing priority values in the several member states; Germany, for example, has given very much less on family benefits but materially more in old-age, death, and survivor benefits than France. Promulgation of a Community-level social policy would require agreement on priorities, and the populations concerned have differing and very deeply held conceptions of how the priorities should be ordered to fit their quality of life. A single system still awaits a political decision in the Community.

While the present European Communities have not imposed a uniform social security system, the Court of Justice has, over nearly two decades, interpreted the treaties to mean that the member states may not take advantage of discrepancies in the existing systems to discriminate, *by reason of nationality*, against *any* Community inhabitant in their jurisdictions. The court's means for exercising its influence are twofold:

1. Under Article 177 of the Treaty of Rome, any member state domestic court court may, in advance of ruling on a case before it that involves any matter covered by the treaty, submit questions to the Court of Justice as to how the language of the treaty should be interpreted. The purpose of the procedure is to bring about an integration of the member states' legal systems to the point where the interpretation on any treaty matter will be uniform in the several national court systems.

2. The Court of Justice has consistently held that the treaty conferred rights directly on individuals and legal persons in the member states without any further enactment by the member states. These rights are subject to enforcement by the courts and are within the jurisdiction of the Court of Justice.[18]

The court's jurisprudence is of special interest in illustrating the creative role envisaged for it.[19] Over the course of its twenty-four–year history the court has reported 979 decisions, which take their place with the treaties as sources of Community law.[20] An increasing use of Article 177 to refer questions from national courts for prejudicial interpretation is reflected in the proportion of such references in the court's docket. The commission's *Seventh General Report on the Activities of the European Communities: 1973* noted this marked trend, which reflects the growing impact of Community law as the national courts are more and more obliged to apply and interpret it.[21] There were 5 referrals in 1968, 16 in 1969, 32 in 1970, 39 in 1971,

40 in 1972, and 61 in 1973. But in 1974 the number was only 39, and in 1975 there were 13 among the 37 cases reported through the end of May. Possibly the enlargement of the Community accounted in part for the unusual increase in 1973 as the courts in new member states tested the procedure, after which the number stabilized. Nevertheless, the requests for preliminary rulings represent a substantial proportion of the total number of judgments currently being published.

Throughout the development of the court's jurisprudence, there has been a persistent undercurrent of positive concern for individual rights and a far-reaching defense of them. The two cases cited at the beginning of this essay illustrate one way in which individuals' rights can be defended by the court. The individuals concerned, of course, represent a very small class; they are employees of one or another of the Community institutions. Any modern bureaucracy, and the European Communities have a well-developed bureaucracy, can be expected to have a machinery for resolving disputes and a final court of appeal. The Court of Justice serves that function. The several agencies of the European Communities have established uniform staff regulations for employees and it was the interpretation of these that occasioned *Airola* v. *Commission* and *Van den Broeck* v. *Commission*.

Cases of that type might be considered of limted impact because they are, in a sense, internal; the Community institutions may set up any staffing standards they and their employees consider reasonable and proscribe such discriminatory practices as they choose. The court has gone further, however; it has said, in *Porrini* v. *EAEC and Comont*, that "the basis of the service relationship between the Community and officials or servants other than local staff cannot reside in a decision of a national court."[22] The advocate general's opinion in the same case asserted that "the national court has no jurisdiction in disputes between the Community and persons who claim the status of officials or that of establishment staff. The European Court of Justice has exclusive jurisdiction to decide such questions."[23] He also cited *Thérèse Vandevyvere* v. *European Parliament* as precedent for including in the Court of Justice's jurisdiction *persons in competitions to become employees* as well as those persons already employed.[24]

This is not to say that the Community is headed for the kind of jurisdictional conflict with national governments which the medieval church encountered over "criminous clerks." While member state authorities may not harass Community employees for performance of their staff duties, their privileges do not include immunity for normal offences in society. In *Sayag* v. *Leduc*, the appellant claimed immunity when charged with damages incurred in an accident while driving an automobile. The court denied the claim, declaring that privileges and immunities did not extend to activities that were merely incidental to the performance of staff duties.[25] Although the court has often seemed to bend over backward in finding favorable interpretations of Community staff regulations for the benefit of individuals against the arbitrariness of superiors and the impersonality of bureaucratic rigidity, there are limits. In *Lepape* v. *High Authority ECSC*, the court awarded the plaintiff, an inspector, reimbursement for the expense of using his own car for official travel during a rail strike but denied a claim for relocation expenses incurred while moving from Luxembourg to Brussels, *when he was transferred by his employer*, because he failed to comply with regulations for securing estimates in advance.[26] And when an employee was just a lazy loafer, as the evidence in *de Vos van Steenwijk* v. *Commission EAEC* plainly showed, he may be, and quite justly was, fired.[27]

So far, the Court of Justice might be seen as simply protecting its own. The cases just cited involved staff personnel in Community agencies. But the court's jurisprudence shows that it has indeed gone equally far in the protection of rights for individuals in the social security cases referred to it from the member states. For the most part the court does not have to protect the nationals of any country in their own system, because the constitutional regimes of the member states offer extensive means for the adjudication of disputes over their own citizens' rights. Problems arise, however, across national social security systems and began early with migrant workers—*migrant workers from other member states*—because the treaties provided for free mobility of labor throughout the territory of the Communities.

Article 48 of the Treaty of Rome required the abolition of discrimination between workers on the ground of nationality, with the general purpose of employing the common labor force of the Community where it was most needed, thus promoting full employment and a stable market. This led to a series of council and commission regulation, and interpretations through court cases, to ensure free circulation of workers.[28] In all these regulations the definition of worker was broadly treated, and the removal of restrictions against aliens entering the labor force ran counter to the common practice of most states under international law. Consequently, workers who were nationals of a member state could compete on equal terms for positions in any area of the Community and move freely to accept jobs, could reside in any member state in order to work there, and could remain after the employment for which they migrated had terminated. The exceptions were chiefly with respect to positions in public administration and jobs which depended specifically on linguistic requirements for performance. Furthermore, foreign workers could bring in their families and could not only join but also vote and hold office in trade unions.

The nub of the problem for free mobility of labor is the social security of the individual worker. Normally, social security legislation applies to individuals in the territory of the legislating unit; if workers who move are penalized in any fashion, their liberty of movement is inhibited. In the extensive litigation occasioned by Community regulations the Court of Justice declared that "Articles 48–51 [of the Treaty of Rome] . . . which constitute the foundation, the framework and the limits of Regulation 3, provide no authority for prohibiting a state from granting additional protection by way of social security to its whole population, including those of its nationals who work in another member country."[29] Rather, "the system adopted by Regulation 3 consists *in abolishing as far as possible the territorial limitations on the application of the different social security schemes.*"[30] In the ten social security cases among the thirty-seven decisions of the court in 1967, most of the questions concerned the calculation of pensions. In these cases the court interpreted Article 51 (qualifying for and retaining benefits) and its implementing regulations as "intended to place the migrant worker in a more favorable situation than that in which he would be placed if domestic law only were to apply."[31] In one of the cases the court interpreted the procedural rules to mean that national courts "may not reject claims or other documents submitted to them, on the grounds that they are written in an official language of another Member State."[32] To make sure that the handicap of differing languages should not work to the disadvantage of migrant workers in their efforts to secure the benefits due them, the court has ruled that with regard to social security claims the method of communicating decisions to workers in another country should be direct and not depend on local national authorities as intermediaries. It has also declared that "notice of a decision adversely affecting the addressee, which if he is abroad, can normally be given by post, is without effect if the instrument is not in a form which enables the addressee to understand it."[33]

Language and nationality differences undoubtedly tangled the web of social security measures. The complexities encountered in harmonizing the different systems of the member states made it difficult to draw up regulations to cover all eventualities by the end of the transitional period that followed the signing of the Treaty of Rome. But the failure of a member state or of a Community agency to take positive action to implement a right envisioned in the Treaty of Rome has not been accepted by the court as a defense for failure to allow it. In *Reyners* v. *Belgium*, Jean Reyners, a Dutch subject born in Brussels, resident there, and educated in Belgium, had been denied registration as an *avocat* because of his non-Belgian nationality. The Treaty of Rome, however, provided that after the end of the transitional period the right of establishment in a business or profession was "a directly applicable provision despite the absence, in a particular sphere, of the directives prescribed by . . . the Treaty."[34] Although the council had not got round to promulgating Community regulations for professions, as it had for workers, Reyners met all the requirements as to professional degrees and training for practicing as an *avocat* imposed in Belgium on Belgians except nationality. Therefore, the court declared he should be registered.

Member states are permitted, under council regulations concerning the movement and residence of foreign nationals dating back to 1964, to take special measures which can be justified on grounds of public policy, public security, or public health. A country could, for example, deport a particular alien who willfully flouted public policy in a manner that country would not tolerate in its own citizens. But the court's interpretation of the regulations stated that the council directive "prevents the deportation of a national of a Member State if such deportation is ordered for the purpose of deterring other aliens."[35] In *Bonsignore* v. *Stadt Köln*, the city of Cologne had ordered the deportation of a young Italian who, about a year earlier, had been involved in an accidental shooting that killed his younger brother. Bonsignore had no criminal record. In the hearings the court found ample evidence that Bonsignore's emotional suffering from the consequences of the accident was heavier punishment than any court had imposed, and there had been no new criminal charge brought against him. At the time of the incident he had not been found guilty of an offense that would cause his deportation. The city's justification of its deportation order after so long a lapse was solely to deter other aliens, and the court ruled that Bonsignore could not legitimately be singled out for that purpose.

The court stated very clearly the relationship between its jurisdiction and that of the legal systems in member states under Article 177 of the Treaty of Rome in *Casagrande* v. *Landeshauptstadt München*, a landmark case in educational rights: "Although under the preliminary rulings procedure the Court cannot judge a national law, it is competent to supply the national court with the principles of interpretation arising from Community law which could guide it in assessing the effects of the national law."[36] This case is of particular interest because it showed the length to which the court's restraint of discrimination on grounds of nationality may go.

Donato Casagrande was born in Munich on December 29, 1953, the son of Italian parents and therefore of Italian nationality. He was still living with his mother in Munich, where his father had been employed before his death in January 1971. Casagrande was enrolled in the Realschule during 1971–72 and applied for the stipend which Munich paid to students in his form when they had insufficient means. His application was refused on the grounds that such stipends were only for Germans, and ultimately a suit over the matter came before the Bayerisches Verfassungsgericht, which asked the Court of Justice for a ruling on interpretation of the applicable Community regulation (Article 12 of Regulation 1612/68). In reply the court's judgment said that, although the competent national authorities must determine the conditions for admission to educational programs and for support, the conditions must not discriminate between children of national workers and of other member state nationals resident in the country. The court's judgment declared:

*Further, since Regulations, under Article 189 of the Treaty, have general application and are binding in their entirety and directly applicable in all Member States, it is irrelevant that the conditions in question are laid down by rules issued by the central power, by the authorities of a country forming part of a Federal State or of other territorial entities, or even by authorities which the national law equates with them. . . . In providing that the children of a national of a Member State who is or has been employed in the territory of another Member State shall be admitted to educational courses "under the same conditions as the nationals" of the host state, Article 12 refers not only to rules relating to admission* but also to general measures intended to facilitate educational attendance.[37]

The court's judgment in *Alaimo v. Préfet du Rhône* extended its interpretation in the Casagrande case to remove financial exigency as an excuse for discrimination by local authorities. Angelo Alaimo, an Italian working in France, applied for a support grant in behalf of his daughter while she attended a training course for which a grant was normally paid. She had been admitted to the course by the school, but the Département du Rhône authorities had decided, because of large numbers of requests, to make grants only to French pupils. The *préfet*'s chief defense was that the local authority had only limited funds and that national grants to aid migrant families became available the following year. In reply to the referral for preliminary ruling the court reaffirmed its earlier judgment. In short, the court of the Communities does not tell local governments how much money they must raise or how to spend it. But the court has ruled that whatever they decide to do with their funds they may not, any more than national governments or Community institutions, discriminate on the basis of nationality among members of the European Community.[38]

The Court of Justice might have confined itself to questions of great economic or political import in the Community: antitrust cases involving multinational corporations, or which Community organ will negotiate for it in treaties involving the Community and outside states where treaty-covered issues are concerned, or nonperformance of treaty obligations by member-states governments.[39] But it did not so limit itself; it *has* been a recourse for the "little fellow." To create a community which people will recognize as their own, it is the rights of the ordinary person, not of the privileged, that want protecting. The European Community is a bureaucracy in which an official at any level can write reports such that another individual may lose his or her job, and the Court of Justice finds time to take the rights of individuals, too, under its wings.

Take, for example, the court's judgment of March 19, 1964, in *Wollast* v. *Commission*. Estelle Wollast was hired by the Commission of the EEC as a nurse for a permanent opening. Pending her integration as a permanent staff member under the comprehensive new staff regulations then being implemented, she received a series of short-term contracts as an auxiliary staff member. At the end of one such contract she was summarily dismissed because of an "incident" reported to her superior. It was alleged that she failed to hurry fast enough when called to the scene of a traffic accident. In court proceedings it became clear that the message about the accident was transmitted to her through a closed door by two messengers "whose mother tongue was neither that of the witness nor of the applicant" while she was administering an injection to a patient. She had answered the call as soon as she finished. Wollast wanted her job back, salary for the time she had not been working (more than a year), and a chance to compete for the permanent job, all of which had been steadily denied to her. The court declared that she should still be under contract and could compete for the permanent job. It also ruled that the defendant commission should pay her back salary, less 15 percent that the court calculated she saved on baby-sitting costs while she was not working, and all costs including reimbursement to the court for legal aid to the applicant.[40]

Time and again the court has found for the beleaguered individual against "the system" and the petty power of bureaucrats. The several institutions of the European Communities have good intentions galore to improve the welfare of individuals.[41] The Economic and Social Committee of the European Communities, for example, declared in October 1975 with respect to the commission's action program for migrant workers—which was directed under treaty provisions only toward migrants from the member states, who make up about one-third of the total of migrant workers, and not to the two-thirds from nonmember states—that "the ultimate aim is to eradicate all discrimination between the two categories, particularly as regards living and working conditions."[42] Such far-reaching changes may come soon or late; the timetable of the council and commission for initiating them is unclear. By comparison, the court's record includes significant concrete contributions; its task is not to provide merely another forum for discussion of the future but to make secure the benefits of those gains already realized.

"Europe will not be built at one stroke, or in a complete structure: it will be built by carrying into effect specific measures, creating to begin with a joint responsibility in fact." These prophetic words from French Minister of Foreign Affairs Robert Schuman's declaration of May 9, 1950, proposing a coal and steel community are graven in stone on a memorial to the French statesman in the city of Luxembourg, underneath a simple inscription: "To Robert Schuman, born at Luxembourg June 29, 1886, initiator of the European Coal and Steel Community, first step toward a united Europe." The memorial stands at the western end of the Grande Duchesse Charlotte Bridge not far from the lofty tower of the European Parliament Secretariat and the new edifice housing the Court of Justice.

The specific steps that will build a united Europe as Schuman envisaged it have begun. How far the building process has progressed may not always be evident, because it is not accomplished at one stroke. The effects of unobserved but inexorable progress, as eighteenth-century revolutionists understood that concept, were poignantly illustrated in a case before the Court of Justice a few years ago.

Antonio Marcato brought suit against the commission because he believed an unfavorable report on his work was unfair. Marcato first went to work for the commission in 1958. On October 1, 1963, he was certified as a computer operator. For the next four years he received uniformly favorable reports in the periodic reviews filed by his superiors. But the review filed in November 1969 was unfavorable; his objections through the complaint procedure of the staff regulations having failed to secure a correction, he went to law. The commission's defense was that, although the plaintiff's qualifications had been adequate at one time, the progress in computer technology was so rapid and had so increased the complexity of the work of operators that the complainant's elementary technical knowledge was insufficient for working with the new equipment in use. He had managed well enough on first-generation computers. But after 1966 the capacity of computers quadrupled in a two-year period. Operators also had to evolve and adapt. Early computers performed operations in sequence; third-generation computers performed multiple simultaneous functions; any operator inadequacy in handling the new capacity compounded the difficulties for others in the computer service. The commission admitted that, as Marcato claimed, he had never failed to do the work assigned him, but this was because his supervisor, recognizing his limits, had not given him work beyond his ability. As the advocate general, a humane gentleman, said before noting the melancholy inevitability of the decision: "M. Marcato is a deserving man. Entering the Commission's service to undertake labor almost entirely physical, he succeeded by his work and his drive in becoming a qualified technician in a particularly ticklish field."[43] But the court could not substitute its judgment for the determination of technical competence required by those responsible for managing the service concerned, and in this case could only adhere to the law: all the proper procedures for review had been correctly followed and the plaintiff's application failed. The changes in his profession had passed him by.

Developments often pass us by and we are unaware of the extent to which they have done so, as with Marcato. A new environment is suddenly there, and we find we cannot put things back the way they were and must adjust to the way things are. Schuman's "Europe" may be evolving faster than its leaders realize. Like all great revolutions, it must be accomplished first in the hearts of men. When it is, the European Community institutions must change too. An essential element of that change will have to be one the court has already recognized: that nationality—the modern corrupted version of fraternity in the old revolutionary trilogy—may not be used to limit liberty and equality.

For it is really national sovereignty that is at the bar. The old vision of the European revolutionary tradition as it was conceived by eighteenth-century intellectuals had no place for artificial barriers to the full enjoyment of the natural rights of individuals. These rights were not different for the French and for the Italians, or the Germans, or any others. The rise of nationalism and the supremacy of the nation-state meant the subordination of the individual to an institution often quite as restrictive of freedom and equality as any under the defunct Old Regime. That society disappeared in violent revolution. To challenge the unlimited sovereignty of the nation-state is as revolutionary in the twentieth century as to attack the divine right of absolute monarchy was in the eighteenth. Perhaps the continued development of revolutionary change will again break into violence over the issue of sovereignty. But the Court of Justice of the European Communities, in asserting the rights of individuals to social justice regardless of nationality, has provided one model for promoting a change which is none the less revolutionary for being nonviolent.

## NOTES

1. Case 21/74 *Airola* v. *Commission* (1975) ECR 221; Case 37/74 *Van den Broeck* v. *Commission* (1975) ECR 235. Owing to the adherence of the United Kingdom, Eire, and Denmark to the Treaty of Rome, the Court of Justice of the European Communities has since 1973 published an English and Danish edition of its reports. These are issued at intervals during the court's term, under the title *Reports of Cases before the Court*, published in Luxembourg, and are cited as European Court Reports (ECR) for the appropriate calendar year. The court had published several volumes, beginning with calendar year 1962, of English translation for prior years; when completed there will be an English-language version corresponding to the previously issued Dutch, French, German, and Italian editions. I have cited the English reports whenever available, otherwise the French, using the form recommended by the court: cases are numbered in the year filed, followed by a name indicating the principals, the year in which decision was reported, the edition (ECR for English), and the page. The pagination is continuous in the reports for any calendar year.
2. Italian law no. 555 of June 13, 1912, provided that "a married woman may not be of different nationality from her husband. . . . An alien who becomes the wife of an Italian citizen acquires Italian nationality." Cited in Case 21/74 *Airola* v. *Commission* (1975) ECR 222.
3. Ibid., p. 221.
4. See, for example, Chalmers Johnson, *Revolution and the Social Sys-*

*tem* (Stanford: Hoover Institute on War, Revolution, and Peace, 1964), and *Revolutionary Change* (London: University of London Press, 1968); Carl J. Friedrich, ed., *Revolution* (New York: Atherton Press, 1967); James H. Meisel, *Counterrevolution: How Revolutions Die* (New York: Atherton Press, 1966); Krishan Kumar, ed., *Revolution: The Theory and Practice of a European Idea* (London: Weidenfeld & Nicholson, 1971); and L. J. Macfarlane, *Violence and the State* (London: Nelson, 1974).

5. Georges Lefebvre, *The Coming of the French Revolution 1789*, trans. R. R. Palmer (Princeton: Princeton University Press, 1949), p. 150. An appendix gives the text of the declaration; see p. 189 for Art. 2, which I have quoted.

6. Jeremy Bentham, *The Limits of Jurisprudence Defined* (New York: Columbia University Press, 1945), p. 85.

7. A. F. Pollard, *England under Protector Somerset: An Essay* (New York: Russell, 1966), p. 204.

8. George Whitecross Paton, *A Text-book of Jurisprudence*, 3d ed., ed. David P. Derham (Oxford: Clarendon Press, 1964), p. 486.

9. Ibid., pp. 488–489.

10. A. D. Hargreaves, *Introduction to the Principles of Land Law*, 4th ed. (London: Sweet & Maxwell, 1963), p. 189.

11. Paton, *Text-book*, p. 488. Paton alludes to the extreme position taken by Léon Duguit in his work, *Les transformations générales du droit privé depuis le code Napoléon* (Paris: F. Alcan, 1912).

12. Paton, *Text-book*, p. 453.

13. See the definition of *patrimoine* in Amos and Walton's *Introduction to French Law*, 3d ed., ed. F. H. Lawson, A. E. Anton, and L. Neville Brown (Oxford: Clarendon Press, 1967), pp. 19–20.

14. Frederic L. Pryor, *Property and Industrial Organization in Communist and Capitalist Nations*, Indiana University International Development Research Center Studies in Development, no. 7 (Bloomington: Indiana University Press, 1973), p. 379.

15. J. E. Meade, *Efficiency, Equality, and the Ownership of Property* (London: George Allen & Unwin, 1964), p. 39.

16. For a reaffirmation of these objectives, see the report pepared by Pierre Maillet et al. for Commission of the European Communities, *Fifteen Years of Community Policy* (Brussels, 1973), p. 6 and passim.

17. Ibid., p. 38.

18. For a discussion of the transfer to the institutions of the European Communities of the exercise of some of the sovereignty of the member states, a transfer not undertaken by the member nations in either the League of Nations or the United Nations, see George Barr Carson Jr., "The Spinning Wheel, the Stone Axe, and Sovereignty," *Canadian Journal of Political Science* 7 (March 1974): 70–85.

19. This role has long been recognized by commentators, for example, Gerhard Bebr, *Judicial Control of the European Communities* (London: Stevens, 1962); E. H. Wall, *The Court of Justice of the European Communities: Jurisprudence and Procedure* (London: Butterworths, 1966); and B. A. Wortley, ed., *An Introduction to the Law of the European Economic Community* (Manchester: Manchester University Press, 1972).

20. According to the Commission of the European Communities, in *Seventh General Report on the Activities of the European Communities: 1973* (Brussels, 1974), p. 480, 775 cases had been decided by the court. The court's periodic *Reports of Cases before the Court* through July 1975 reported an additional 204 cases.

21. Commission, *Seventh General Report*, p. 69.

22. Case 65/74 *Porrini v. EAEC and Comont* (1975) ECR 330.

23. Ibid., p. 335.

24. Case 23/64 *Thérèse Vandevyvere v. European Parliament* (1964) ECR 157.

25. Case 5/68 *Sayag v. Leduc* (1968) ECR 395.

26. Case 11/63 *Lepape v. High Authority ECSC* (1964) ECR 61.

27. Case 84/63 *de Vos van Steenwijk v. Commission EAEC* (1964) ECR 321.

28. A detailed listing of these cases can be found in K. Lipstein, *The Law of the European Community* (London: Butterworths, 1974), pp. 84–92. The key regulation was Council Reg. 3 of September 25, 1958, *Official Journal of the European Communities [OJ]* (Brussels), 1958, 561, with supplementary provisions in Council Reg. 4 of December 3, 1958, *OJ*, 1958, 597, and numerous subsequent amendments in details. Reg. 3 was replaced by Council Reg. 1408/71 of June 14, 1971, *OJ*, 1971, L 149/2.

29. Case 92/63 *Nonnenmacher v. Sociale Versekeringsbank* (1964) ECR 290.

30. Case 44/65 *Hessische Knappschaft v. Singer* (1965) ECR 971

(my italics).

31. Commission of the European Communities, *First General Report on the Activities of the European Communities: 1967* (Brussels, 1968), p. 437.

32. Case 6/67 *Pace* v. *Assurance Maladie-Invalidité* (1967) ECR 219.

33. Case 66/74 *Farrauto* v. *Bau-Berufsgenossenschaft* (1975) ECR 168. Anyone who has coped with bureaucratese can sympathize with the Italian worker's problems over a notification in German about his pension claims.

34. Case 2/74 *Reyners* v. *Belgium* (1974) ECR 631.

35. Case 67/74 *Bonsignore* v. *Stadt Köln* (1975) ECR 308.

36. Case 9/74 *Casagrande* v. *Landeshauptstadt München* (1974) ECR 774.

37. Ibid., p. 780 (my italics).

38. Case 68/74 *Alaimo* v. *Préfet du Rhône* (1975) ECR 109.

39. Some recent examples of these categories of dispute are Case 6/72 *Europemballage and Continental Can* v. *Commission* (1973) ECR 215; CJEC 31 March 1971 (*Commission* v. *Council*, Case 22-70) Recueil, 1971, 263; and Case 12/74 *Commission* v. *Germany* (1975) ECR 181.

40. Case 18/63 *Wollast* v. *Commission* (1964) ECR 85.

41. See, for example, Commission President F.-X. Ortoli, *Eighth General Report on the Activities of the European Communities: 1974* (Brussels, 1975), p. LXI; "Reports on European Union," *Bulletin of the European Communities* (Brussels, 1975), Supplements 5/75 and 9/75; Economic and Social Committee of the European Communities, *Annual Report 1974* (Brussels, 1975).

42. *Bulletin of the Economic and Social Committee of the European Communities*, no. 10 (October 1975), p. 23.

43. CJEC 17 March 1971 (Marcato/Commission, 29–70) Recueil, 1971, 249. The advocate general was the late Dutheillet de Lamothe.